THE WORLD

OF

BUDGERIGARS

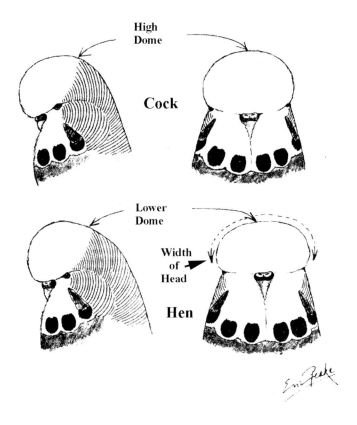

Drawn by Eric Peake
for *The Cult of the Budgerigar*

BUDGERIGAR TITLES

Homing Budgerigars
Duke of Bedford

Inbreeding Budgerigars
Dr M D S Armour

World of Budgerigars
Cyril H Rogers

Cult of the Budgerigar
W Watmough
Revised by James Blake
Probably the most famous of all books published
on the budgerigar.

The Budgerigar Book
Ernest Howson
Revised by James Blake

THE WORLD

OF

BUDGERIGARS

CYRIL H. ROGERS, FBSA

Revised by James Blake

Northbrook Publishing Ltd
Beech Publishing House
Station Yard
Elsted Marsh
Midhurst
West Sussex GU209 0JT

ISBN 1-85736-270-5

First published 1981

Second Edition 1987

Third Edition 1990

Fourth Edition 1999

Fifth Edition 2001

British Library Cataloguing-in-Publication Data
A catalogue record for this book is available
from the British Library.

Northbrook Publishing Ltd
Beech Publishing House
Station Yard
Elsted Marsh
Midhurst
West Sussex GU209 0JT

Printed by Warwick Printing Company Limited,
Theatre Street, Warwick CV34 4DR

CONTENTS

MONOCHROME ILLUSTRATIONS

LIST OF COLOURED PLATES

Between pages 22 and 23. The 24 plates show the early types as well as modern birds. Illustrations are based on paintings by Eric Peake, R A Vowles and Frances Fry (after R A Vowles, and a photograph of Spangles supplied by the author.

ACKNOWLEDGEMENTS

We should like to thank the **Budgerigar Society** for allowing the reproduction of their Ideal Birds, tables of Standards and Standard Cages.

In addition we should like to acknowledge the following as sources of illustrations:

The Cult of the Budgerigar by W. Watmough
The Budgerigar in Bush and Aviary by Neville W. Cayley, FRZS
Illustrated Natural History by Reverend J.G. Woods
Budgerigars and Cockatiels by C.P. Arthur
Exhibition Budgerigars by Dr. M.D.S. Armour
Illustrations of the British Flora by Fitch and Smith
Avicultural Magazine 4th Series, Vol. III
Autosomal Colour Mosaics in the Budgerigar (Journal of Genetics III) by F.A.E. Crew and Rowena Lamy
A Lecture on Mendelism by Drinkwater
The Budgerigar in Captivity by Denys Weston

PREFACE

Although there have been many excellent books written over the years on the keeping, breeding and exhibiting of Budgerigars, they only touch very briefly on parts of their history and development as a wild and a domesticated species. However, in this book I have endeavoured to collate all the available information from avicultural literature and my private records and memories since these delightful birds were first introduced into Europe. During the past decade or two I have, in my capacity as Budgerigar correspondent to *Cage and Aviary Birds* and other Journals, been constantly asked for particulars of when certain mutations appeared, who first bred them, when *standard* show cages were adopted, when closed metal rings were obligatory for Breeder's classes and a host of other questions appertaining to all of the Budgerigar Fancy. I sincerely hope that Fanciers will find that the majority of their questions are answered in the pages of this book.

Cyril H. Rogers.
Aldringham, Suffolk, 1981.

Frontispiece Habitat of the Wild Budgerigar — virgin forest near Melbourne, Australia

From *The Cult of the Budgerigar* W. Watmough

CHAPTER 1

DISCOVERY IN THE WILD AND EARLY BREEDINGS

CLASSIFICATION AND THE NATURALISTS

There have been many and varied names given to the Budgerigar since it was first discovered by a European, John Gould, in Australia, in 1794. The following provides a comprehensive list of these names, beginning with the Latin classifications of the breed varieties, as given by the early Naturalists, notably Gould, Shaw and Nodder, and Mathews.

Budgerigar
1. *Melopsittacus undulatus undulatus* (Shaw and Nodder)
   Subspecies — *M.u. intermedius* and *M.u. pallidceps*
2. *Psittacus undulatus* (Shaw and Nodder 1805)
3. *Melopsittacus* (Gould 1840)

Names adopted in other countries:

Australia — Shell Parrots, Shellie, Budgerigar
U.S.A. — Parakeet, Budgerigar
Germany — Wellensittich
France — Perruche ondulee
Netherlands — Grasparkiet
Sweden — Undulater

Alternative names used in the past:
Undulated Parrakeet, Zebra Parrakeet, Warbling Grass Parrakeet, Grass Parrot, Waved Parrot, Canary Parrot and Scallop Parrot.

Native Aboriginal names:
Padda-moora, Pa-thara, Kilykilyhari, Betcherry-gah and Budgery-gah.

The native names vary somewhat according to the district where the tribes of Aborigines live. In one area, the first part of the now universal name Budgerigar means 'good', and the last syllable indicates 'food' or 'to eat'. This shows that Budgerigars were 'good to eat' and undoubtedly they formed part of the diet of the tribe. To support this I quote from Neville W. Cayley's, F.R.Z.S.., *Budgerigar in Bush and Aviary* (1933).

One of the early teachings of the Aboriginal youth was to locate the whereabouts of food supplies, and it was not long before the breeding ground of the Budgerigar was visited. When the young were about in the fledging stage every log and spout was raked and probed with sticks, the squeaking young dragged out. These were quickly roasted at convenient fires and the juicy morsels eagerly devoured.

Subspecies

Mr.Cayley's book also contains many most interesting reports from ornithological observers of wild Budgerigars in various areas of Australia:

(a) *M.u. intermedius* (Mathews) similar in colour to *M.u. undulatus*, but of a paler shade, especially on the neck and back areas. This subspecies is apparently confined to the Northern Territory.

(b) *M.u. pallidiceps* (Mathews) again similar to *M.u. undulatus*, except that the head colouring is much paler in tone. These paler headed birds are found in the vast ranges of Western Australia; their exact location does not seem to have been pin-pointed by any observers.

These two subspecies, as identified by Mathews, are, apparently, not recognised as such by other Naturalists. Most Australian Budgerigar Fanciers seem to think that the slight variations in shade of colour found among the wild birds of the various States are too small to constitute any true subspecies. There is, however, undoubtedly *a* difference in colour shades of birds coming from these special areas, and these slight differences can be noted in some of our present day domesticated strains.

Nesting habits

Like most Parrot-like birds, Budgerigars do not build nests in the true sense, but use holes in trees, which the hens excavate and enlarge to make into suitable nesting chambers. The trees mostly favoured are the large Eucalyptus and Mulga, but they will use other trees in their breeding area which have the hollow bowls so suitable for the birds' purpose. Nest holes of other species, such as Woodpeckers, are also used by Budgerigars if they are present in trees in their nesting areas.

Four to six white **eggs** (17.2-19.1 mm x 14.1-15.0 mm in size) are laid, and incubation lasts for eighteen days for each egg; as the eggs are laid on alternate days there is thus a difference between the hatching of the first and last egg of the clutch. It is only the hen bird that incubates, although her mate feeds her on the nest and shares the duties of rearing the

Figure 1.1   Early Type of an Exhibition Budgerigar

young. The young leave the nest fully feathered when they are approximately four weeks old and remain in the care of their parents for a further period of about ten days or so. A further clutch of eggs are usually laid about the time the last young of the first brood are leaving the nest hollow.

Distribution

Most of Australia with the population density increasing in the inland areas. *M.u. intermedius* is confined to the Northern Territory and *M.u. pallidiceps* to Western Australia.

Description
Cock

Front of head yellow; throat (mask) yellow, ornamented on each side with three round black spots, the back ones partially covered by a bright blue cheek flash. Back of head, nape of neck, mantle and wings yellowish, heavily marked with narrow black barring which becomes broader on the wings and back and more brownish in tone. Flight and secondaries brownish-black, marked with white in the middle of the centre webs.

Tail: the two long central feathers dark blue with a greenish tinting on the outer edges towards the face, remaining feathers greenish-blue with yellow markings.

Body: bright grass green, rump, undertail coverts and thighs rich grass green.

Beak: greyish-horn.

Cere: shiny blue.

Eyes: dark with pale yellow iris ring.

Feet and legs: greyish-blue

Length approximately 7½-8 inches (19.05-20.32 cm).

Hen

Coloured similarly but slightly duller in overall appearance to the cock, except the cere is chocolate brown and rough (whitish blue and smooth when out of breeding condition).

Immature

A duller colour, but otherwise like adults, with barring on the head extending down to the cere and some faint barring possibly appearing on the chest near wing butts.

Cere: pale whitish-blue.

Eyes: dark without the light iris ring. This light ring does not appear until a bird is a few months old.

Feet and legs: dull blue.

4

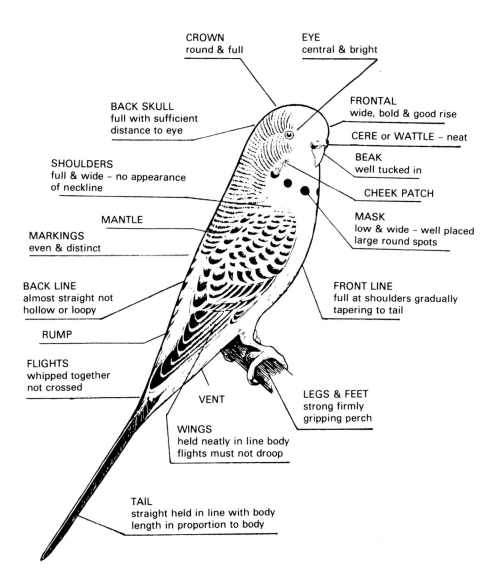

CROWN
round & full

EYE
central & bright

BACK SKULL
full with sufficient
distance to eye

FRONTAL
wide, bold & good rise

CERE or WATTLE – neat

BEAK
well tucked in

SHOULDERS
full & wide – no appearance
of neckline

CHEEK PATCH

MASK
low & wide – well placed
large round spots

MANTLE

MARKINGS
even & distinct

BACK LINE
almost straight not
hollow or loopy

FRONT LINE
full at shoulders gradually
tapering to tail

RUMP

FLIGHTS
whipped together
not crossed

VENT

LEGS & FEET
strong firmly
gripping perch

WINGS
held neatly in line body
flights must not droop

TAIL
straight held in line with body
length in proportion to body

Figure 1.2   Main Features of a Budgerigar

Figure 1.3 The first published illustration of a Budgerigar, from Shaw and Nodder'
Naturalists' Miscellany.

6

EARLY HISTORY

It would seem that an accurate description of the Budgerigar was first given by the naturalists Shaw and Nodder in their *Naturalists' Miscellany* published between the last decade of the 1800's and the first of the 1900's (now out of print). The picture of the engraving (see opposite) under the description of *Psittacus undulatus* accompanied their notes.

The next account appears in the *Naturalists' Library* Vol.X by Sir William Jardine and P.J. Selby published in the 1820's (out of print). The colour tinted plate by Lear, showing the Budgerigar under the name of *Nanodes undulatus*, contained in that volume, is far less accurate in its portrayal of a Budgerigar than that of Shaw & Nodder (see page 8).

Undoubtedly John Gould's *Birds of Australia and adjacent Islands* (1837)* contains the best early plate of Budgerigars, depicting in precise detail a true pair and an immature bird in his usual pleasing style. Several other naturalists of that period, including Wagler, Lear, Vigors and Horsfield, added further information to the general picture of the wild Green Budgerigar.

A Budgerigar skin was placed in the Linnean Society's Museum, London, as early as 1831, although actual live birds were nor brought to Europe until 1840, as recorded by C. H. Rogers in *Budgerigars* (1970)** from which I quote:

> . . . in 1840 the first record of living specimens coming into Great Britain including into Europe was made by John Gould. These birds were brought over by John Gould the world famous naturalist and artist; and it was his brother-in-law, Charles Coxon, who reared the first Budgerigars in captivity. Some old writers say that this first breeding took place in Australia and others that it happened in Great Britain, but wherever it was Charles Coxon appears to be the first breeder....

First British Breeding

With all probability, the first Budgerigars to be bred in Great Britain came from the birds imported by John Gould, although other examples must have come into this country and Europe within a short time of the arrival of Gould's birds. According to Arthur T.A. Prestwick in his *Records of Parrots bred in captivity* Part VI (1952) the earliest printed records he could find were in the Zoological Gardens reports for 1857-60. In the *Zoologist* (1859), it was noted that a Mrs. E.A. Eeles of Southwold, Suffolk, had been successful in rearing four young Green Budgerigars in a Canary breeding cage. What appears to be the first advertisement offering British bred Budgerigars for sale appeared in the

*Published in four Volumes or Handbook by Lansdowne Press

**Published by Bartholomew, Foyle, Gifford and Magna Print Books.

Figure 1.4 Budgerigar drawn by Lear from Jardine and Selby's *Naturalists' Library*

Figure 1.5 Group of Budgerigars, from Gould's *Birds of Australia and the adjacent Islands*

9

Field of April 1859, where a Mr. T.Moore of Fareham, Hants, offered a pair of English bred Shell Paraquets (Budgerigars) for £2.

EARLY WRITERS

The Reverend J.G. Woods' *Illustrated Natural History,* published in 1862 gives a detailed description of the Warbling Grass Parrakeet, to accompany the illustration which is reproduced here opposite.

One of the very prettiest and most interesting of the Parrot tribe is the Grass or Zebra Parrakeet; deriving its names from its habits and the markings of its plumage.

It is a native of Australia, and may be found in almost all the central portions of that land, whence it has been imported in such great numbers as an inhabitant of our aviaries, that when Dr. Bennett was last in England, he found that he could purchase the birds at a cheaper rate in England that in New South Wales. This graceful little creature derives its name of Grass Parrakeet from its fondness for the grass lands, where it may be seen in great numbers, running amid the thick grass blades, clinging to their stems, or feeding on their seeds. It is always an inland bird, being very seldom seen between the mountain ranges and the coasts.

Of the habits of this bird Mr. Gould writes as follows: "I found myself surrounded by numbers, breeding in all the hollow spouts of the large Eucalypti bordering the Mokai; and on crossing the plains between that river and the Peel, in the direction of the Turi mountains, I saw them in flocks of many hundreds, feeding upon the grass seeds that are there abundant. So numerous were they, that I determined to encamp upon the spot, in order to observe their habits and to procure specimens. The nature of their food and the excessive heat of these planes compel them frequently to seek the water; hence my camp, which was pitched near some small fords, was constantly surrounded by large numbers, arriving in flocks varying from twenty to a hundred or more.

The hours at which they were most numerous were early in the morning, and some time before dark in the evening. Before going down to drink, they alight on the neighbouring trees, settling together in clusters, sometimes on the dead branches, and at others on the drooping boughs of the Eucalypti. Their flight is remarkably straight and rapid, and is generally accompanied by a screeching noise. During the heat of the day, when sitting motionless among the leaves of the gum-trees, they so closely assimilate in colour, particularly on the breast, that they are with difficulty detected."

The voice of this bird is quite unlike the rough screeching sounds in which Parrots seem to delight, and is a gentle, soft, warbling kind of song, which seems to be contained within the body, and is not poured out with that decision which is usually found in birds that can sing, however small their efforts may be. This song, if it may be so called, belongs only to the male bird, who seems to have an idea that his voice must be very agreeable to his mate, for in light warm weather he will warble nearly all day long, and often pushes his beak almost into the ear of his mate, so as to give her the full benefit of his song. The lady, however, does not seem to appreciate his condescension as he wishes, and sometimes pecks him sharply in return. Dr. Bennett observes that the bird has some ventriloquial powers, as he has noticed a Grass Parrakeet engaged in the amusement of imitating two birds, one warbling and the other chirping.

In its native land it is a migratory bird, assembling after the breeding season in enormous flocks as a preparation for their intended journey. The general number of the eggs is three or four, and they are merely laid in the holes of the gum-tree without requiring a nest.

Figure 1.6 Warbling Grass Parrakeet

The general colour of this pretty bird is dark mottled green, variegated with other colours. The forehead is yellow, and the head, the nape of the neck, the upper part of the back, the scapularies and the wing-coverts are light yellowish green, each feather being marked with a crescent-shaped spot of brown near the tip, so as to produce the peculiar mottling so characteristic of the species. These markings are very small on the head, and increase in size on the back, and from their shape the bird is sometimes called the Shell or Scallop Parrot. On each cheek there is a patch of deep blue, below which are three circular spots of the same rich hue. The wings are brown, having their outer webs deep green, roped with a yellower tint. The throat is yellow, and the abdomen and whole under surface light grass-green. The two central tail-feathers are blue, and the remainder green, each with an oblique band of yellow in the middle.

The young birds have the scallopings all over the head, and the females are coloured almost exactly like their mate, who may be distinguished by the cere of the upper part of the beak being of a deep purple.

Cassell's *Book of Birds,* translated from the original text of Dr. Brehm, Germany, by T. Rymer Jones, F.R.C., and published towards the end of the nineteenth century, also contains much interesting information on the Budgerigar, under the name of **Waved Parrot:**

They came in flocks of from twenty to one hundred to a small lake to drink, and from this locality flew at stated times over the plain in search of the seeds which are their exclusive food; they went to the water in the greatest numbers in the early morning or as it grew dark in the evening. During the heat of the day they sat motionless under the leaves of the gum-trees ... Their activity is wonderful, and their flight very rapid resembling that of a falcon or swallow; they run upon the ground with facility, but their feet are ill adapted for climbing amongst the branches of trees ... As soon as breeding time is over, the flocks begin their migrations, during which they pass regularly from south to north, and only return to their breeding places when the grass seeds are ripe ... In the Spring of 1861, two pairs of these birds flew from a cage to the estate of a noted collecter in Belgium; they betook themselves to the tops of some high trees in a large park, and were lost during some time. While they remained at large, as it afterwards proved, they made their nest and reared a number of young ones.

Dr. Karl Russ was another German writer on ornithology of about the same time as Dr. Brehm, and he gives a good account of early breedings in Europe. For his information on their wild life, he quotes freely from Gould's earlier field material. His work *The Budgerigar* was translated into English at the end of the last century. In this book, incidentally, Russ related how a lady had trained a Budgerigar to imitate the human voice. This was the first time such an achievement had been officially recorded, although Budgerigars, being Parrot-like birds, always held this promise.

Early Breeders

Amongst the early breeders of Budgerigars in Great Britain was C.P. Arthur who bred them during the last decades of the 1900's and the first part of the twentieth century. Mr. Arthur has the distinction of being the first person in Great Britain to produce a **Lutino** (Red-eyed Clear

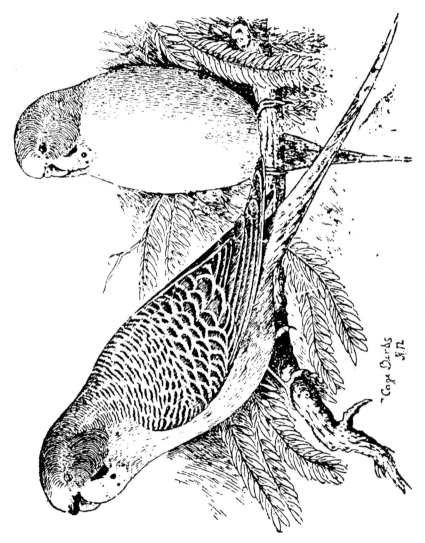

"Cage Birds"
J.R.

Figure 1.7   An early drawing of domestic Budgerigars

Yellow) Budgerigar. Although there had been a number of useful articles on Budgerigars both in their captive state and in the wild, Mr. Arthur was the first British author of a small book giving many details of their housing, feeding, breeding and health. I quote some items of interest from Mr. Arthur's book *Budgerigars and Cockatiels*:

> **Budgerigars live to be a good old age. I know of two cock birds which lived together in a canary's 'hang up' cage for twenty two years. These were some of the importation of 1879. Over fifty thousand pairs were imported into England during the first six months of that year, when they were sold at a guinea a dozen. But they were nearly all cocks; I had several dozen and there was not a hen amongst them . . . Speaking of hot water reminds me of a curious thing which happened regarding my pair of pink-eyed Lutino Budgerigars, and which made me think I had discovered a way of producing Lutinos. But whether my action had anything to do with it I must leave scientists to say. Looking round the husks to see that all was going on right I noticed in this particular husk — which was near the ground, as the cock bird could not fly well — three eggs, two of which were quite covered with excrement from the last nest of young . . . I put a spoon into the husk and brought out the two eggs which I dropped into a basin of hot water. My wife's attention for the moment was taken up with some other inmates of the aviary. She then happened to look round, and seeing what I had done, instantly exclaimed 'Charlie, you will kill those eggs, the water was boiling when I brought it out'. I whipped them out and wiped them clean and put them back into the nest never dreaming they would hatch. But they did. Strange as it may seem these two eggs produced what I believe to be the only Lutino Budgerigars ever known . . . I am afraid to say how many eggs I have since spoiled in experiments, but without producing any more Lutinos.**

In the above quotation it will be noticed that the work 'husk' is used; this husk is the fibrous case of the coconut. In the early days of Budgerigar breeding coconut husks were used as nests — the husk was split in halves lengthways, one end of a half was cut off and the two pieces wired together forming a covered hollow nest.

I know that readers will be surprised to learn from the quotation of the considerable numbers of Budgerigars imported from Australia at that time, nearly one hundred years ago. Although there were plenty of birds in this country, and Europe, their breeding must have been somewhat limited, because of the extreme shortage of hen birds. It can be wondered whether this was by design, to prevent free breeding in aviaries, or whether cock birds were easier for the trappers to catch.

It is certainly rather a strange happening that the two eggs that were immersed for a time in very hot water produced two red-eyed Lutino chicks. In his book Mr. Arthur did not state the sex of these Lutinos although he does say they would not breed together but did so with normal Greens. From this statement it could be surmised that both birds were hens and naturally would not breed when put together. On the other hand, he stated they bred with Greens, and if one had been a cock of the sex-linked Lutino kind some Lutino hens would surely have

14

resulted from the cross. Should they have been non-linked Lutinos then even if one was a cock only green-coloured chicks would have been obtained. The other probability is that the sudden shock of being plunged into nearly boiling water at a certain stage of their development caused the colour change, which was not of an inheritable nature, but due to an outside physical cause. There is no need nowadays for any breeders to waste eggs on such experiments, as Lutinos are quite plentiful.

WILD CAUGHT BUDGERIGARS

The last consignment of wild caught Australian Budgerigars was imported on a special licence into Great Britain at the end of 1934 by Major J.S.S. Clarke of Clevedon, Somerset. These birds were used as a pure basis for testing mutant colours and generally strengthening the domestic strains. I quote the following observation from Major Clarke's Article in the *Budgerigar Bulletin* No. 32 of 1934:

> **Readers will naturally like to know what these birds are like. They are small, but their colour does not seem to be very far off that of our own light greens. They are very vivacious and active — in fact so active that I cannot count them yet. Their shape seems good and, if there is one thing more certain than anything else the gentleman who wrote in** *Cage Birds* **about the 'rather gaudy wild bird' was talking through his hat about a subject of which he was entirely ignorant.**

This is, I think, the first comparison to be made between the wild caught and the domestic exhibition types of Budgerigars.

Just prior to Major Clarke's consignment of wild Green Budgerigars from Australia, John Marsden of Haysham, Lancs, had obtained a few pairs of Australian Greens for his experiments. Mr. Marsden was an early enthusiast of Budgerigar breeding and exhibiting and is perhaps best known for his opposition to the Mendelian theory (see Chapter 2) and his support for the 'Blue-bred' idea. I can remember seeing examples of both these importations and they were more slender, somewhat smaller headed, tighter in feather and more even in colour than most of the domesticated Greens of that time.

With the cessation of the importation of wild caught Budgerigars, first through the lack of demand because of the increased availability of cheap aviary bred stock of better exhibition type and later by an Australian Government Ban on the export of live birds, Budgerigars took on a new status. This change, together with the increase in mutant colours, quickly led to a dramatic development in Budgerigars as cage and aviary birds.

15

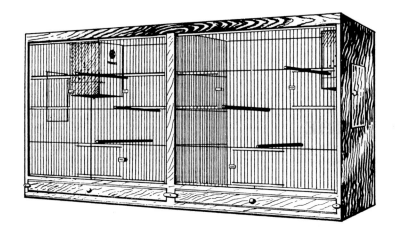

Figure 2.1   Budgerigar Double Breeding Cage with Nest-boxes in position

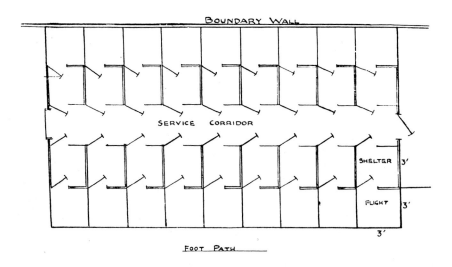

Figure 2.2   Ground Plan of Breeding Block

16

CHAPTER 2

THE DEVELOPMENT OF THE DOMESTICATED BUDGERIGAR

EARLY EXHIBITION

Until the latter part of the nineteenth century Budgerigars were coming to Great Britain mainly from their native country, but their numbers were being augmented by small quantities of European and British bred stock. A few birds found their way to the larger Cage Bird Exhibitions where they were shown in true pairs either in mixed Parrakeet classes or in special classes for Australian Grass Parrakeets, as Budgerigars were often called. In about 1877 classes were scheduled for Budgerigar pairs and up to twenty-nine entries appeared in these classes at big shows.

At the turn of the century there was somewhat of a decline in the support of the Budgerigar classes and consequently show promoters often amalgamated Budgerigars with other Parrakeets. During this period a few Yellows, in addition to the ordinary Greens, were being shown against strong competition from other Parrot-like species.

In 1910, avicultural history was made when Mons. R. Pauwels of Belgium exhibited a pair of Sky Blues in a mixed class at a show held in the old Horticultural Hall, London. Just prior to World War I there was an awakening of interest in Budgerigars and separate classes for them were again being scheduled. Unfortunately progress in this direction was stopped during the war years of 1914-1919, both here and on the Continent.

Soon after the war was over the breeding and showing of Budgerigars started once more in earnest with a number of new mutations appearing, to add to the already growing interest in these delightful little Parrakeets. There was a steady rise in the number of people keeping and breeding Budgerigars both for pleasure and exhibition purposes, and much more detailed information was being published in the Fancy Press and Societies' magazines by the keen and successful breeders of that time. It was during this period that I obtained my first pairs of Light Green and Light Yellow Budgerigars.

THE BUDGERIGAR CLUB

In fact the cult of keeping Budgerigars was growing so fast that in 1925, at the Crystal Palace Exhibition of Cage Birds, London, a group of these dedicated Budgerigar Fanciers got together and founded the **Budgerigar Club**, the first Specialist Club for the development of Budgerigars. Amongst the founder members were Allen Silver, Herbert Whitley, John Frostick, John Marsden, Fred Longlands, Denys Weston, R.J. Watts, C.P. Arthur, H. Tod Boyd, T.C. Charlton, Capt. G.E. Rattigan, myself and others.

The first officers of the Club were Herbert Whitley, President, Allen Silver Chairman, Fred Longlands Hon. Secretary and Treasurer, with a good supporting committee of enthusiastic breeders, who together formulated the initial working rules and a standard show cage. In February of the following year the first Club Show was staged at the Crystal Palace, London, with nine classes and one hundred entries judged by R.J. Watts of Cambridge. Shortly after the establishment and progression of the **Budgerigar Club**, the Japanese boom in Budgerigars started raising some fears about the effect that the tremendously high prices offered and the uncontrollable development in mass breeding would have on the Budgerigar as an exhibition bird.

Early Prices

For a short period the prices offered for the rarer colours were quite fantastic, when the contemporary value of the pound is considered. At the peak of the demand, the prices offered and paid by dealers were; Sky Blues £100-£125, Cobalts £150-£175, Mauves (Lilacs) £175, Whites £200, with one pair of Whites said to have gone to Japan for £1,000, and Greens and Yellows fetching £4-£6 per pair. Fortunately fears were not realised and as the craze in Japan receded and prices became realistic once again, Budgerigar keeping went steadily ahead. The boom however did have one good effect because it had interested many more people in breeding Budgerigars and a good number continued in the Fancy after the Japanese market dried up.

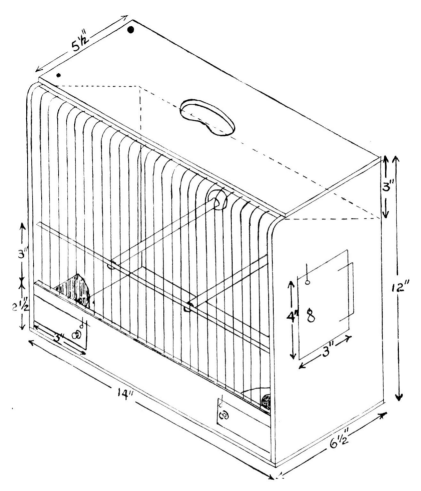

The illustration herewith is that of the type of cage adopted by
your Committee as the standard for the exhibition of Budgerigars by the members of the Club. The cage may be painted to
individual taste, and the material used for covering the bottom
of the cage is also optional.

Exhibits in any other type of cage will be accepted for ordinary
competition, but will not be eligible to compete for any of the
Club specials at Shows held under Club patronage.

FRED C. LONGLANDS
Hon. Sec.

Figure 2.3   The first Standard Show Cage, 1936
courtesy: **The Budgerigar Society**

19

CLUB SHOW ENTRIES

The steady growth of **The Budgerigar Club** can be measured to some extent by looking at the entries at the Club Show from 1926 to 1935. In 1926, as already stated, there were 100 entries; in 1927, 171 entries; in 1928, 131 entries; in 1929, 252 entries; in 1930, 345 entries; in 1931, 414 entries; in 1932, 560 entries; in 1933; 723 entries; in 1934, 1119 entries; in 1935, 958 entries and in 1936, 1130 entries, with the Champion Light Green cocks totalling 68; hens 52; Novice 59 cocks and 25 hens. The competition in those days was certainly keen and very strong and at the present time it is rare to see classes so well supported even at the larger shows.

Obviously there must be sound reasons for the surge in popularity of Budgerigar breeding and exhibiting, in addition to the good publicity stemming from the Japanese boom. At that time the **Budgerigar Club** did much to standardise the Budgerigar as an efficient exhibition breed and published in its *Bulletin* a large amount of specialised information on breeding. This work brought an excellent response from fanciers both at home and overseas and gave the hobby a further boost. Another important factor, this time a natural one, was the appearance of numerous colour mutations in various parts of the world. These new colours provided more interest in breeding which was being developed on scientific lines to the lasting benefit of the Bird Fancy as a whole. The various colour mutations and their composite forms will be found discussed in detail in other chapters.

So that readers can assess for themselves the progress of the domesticated Budgerigar as an exhibition bird the following information from the various periods is provided.

Scale of Points

The 1925 *Year Book of the Budgerigar Club* contained a scale of points to assist judges and exhibitors to assess the quality of the birds. The scale below is interesting to compare with that in current use for the same colours today:

Variety	Condition	Colour	Spots	Type	Size	Total
Green	50	20	10	5	15	100
Yellow	50	30	5	5	10	100
Light Blue	50	30	5	5	10	100
Dark Blue	50	30	5	5	10	100

As the number of colours increased, the scale of points list was suitably extended and at the end of the 1930's it was as indicated on page 23.

It is also enlightening to note that closed, coded, numbered and year dated metal rings were being offered for sale to members by one of the present day **Budgerigar Society's** ring makers, Messrs. Hughes of Hampton Hill, Middlesex.

Close Ringing

At the Annual General Meeting of the **Budgerigar Club** held on 7th February 1931 at the Crystal Palace Exhibition, London, the use of closed coded year dated metal rings for young birds was discussed at great length. A proposal was put forward that only young birds wearing these rings should be eligible for the Young Bird classes. Strange as it may seem today this proposal was defeated and the use of closed coded rings for birds in Young Bird classes did not come into force until 1934. At the A.G.M. of February 1932 it was agreed that *no* new trophies be accepted for competition as Breeders Trophies, unless they were confined to birds wearing closed coded metal rings issued to the breeder by the official ring makers. It was in 1935 that the first closed coded year dated *coloured* rings were evolved.

Standard Show Cage

In the following year, 1936, the *Year Book* contained an illustration with dimensions of the standard show cage (see Illustration page 9). With the exception of a few small modifications, the cage was the same as our present day *standard* and this does credit to the forethought of the original designers; it was based on particulars submitted to the committee by Allen Silver.

Although the first approved drawing of an ideal Budgerigar was not depicted until 1937 and appeared in the December issue of the *Budgerigar Bulletin* No. 44 a photograph of a Crystal Palace Club Show winning Sky Blue cock was in the June issue 1930 of the *Budgerigar Bulletin* No. 13. These give an excellent idea of the type of exhibition Budgerigars of that period. Plates of these two birds will be found on pages 22 and 25.

ROYAL PATRONAGE

During the period of development of the Budgerigar now under discussion a very important event took place which had a profound effect on the **Budgerigar Club**. This extract from the *Budgerigar Bulletin* No. 12 of March gives a complete picture:

> **It is my great pleasure to announce that His Majesty the King has most graciously consented to become Patron of our Society.**
> **I was privileged to ask for this favour and received a reply that His Majesty had**

Figure 2.4   The Ideal Budgerigar, 1937, and Scale of Points
courtesy: **The Budgerigar Society**

22

Plate 1. Early Illustration of Budgerigars

Mauve	Grey	Blue
Yellow	White	Olive
	Green	

Plate 2. First Colour Plate of Bi-colours or Half-siders

Plate 3. A Year 1935, Cobalt Cock; an Ideal specimen at that time.

Plate 4. Yellow-wing Dark Green (Modern Type)

Plate 5. Lutino Cock (Old Style)

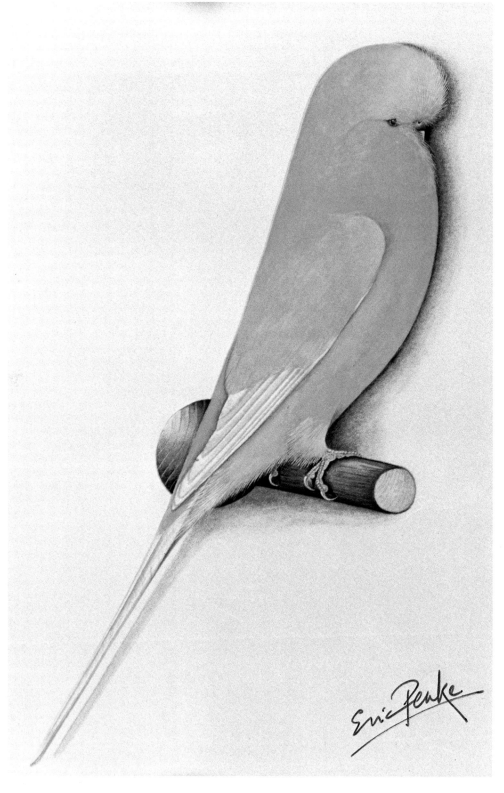

Plate 6. Lutino Cock (Modern Type)

Plate 7. Light Green Cock (Old Style)

Plate 8. Light Green Cock (Modern Type)

Plate 9. Skyblue Cock (Old Style)

Plate 10. Skyblue Cock (Modern Type)

Plate 11. Grey Cock and Grey Hen (Old Style)

Plate 12.   Grey Cock (Modern Type)

Plate 13. Opaline Blue Hen & Opaline Light Green Cock (Old Style)

Plate 14. Opaline Light Green (Modern Type)

Plate 15. Violet Cock & Cobalt Hen (Old Style)

Plate 16. Violet Cock (Modern Type)

Plate 17. Grey Pied (Modern Type)

Plate 18. Whitewing Cobalt (Modern Type)

Plate 19. Recessive Pied (Green) [Modern Type]

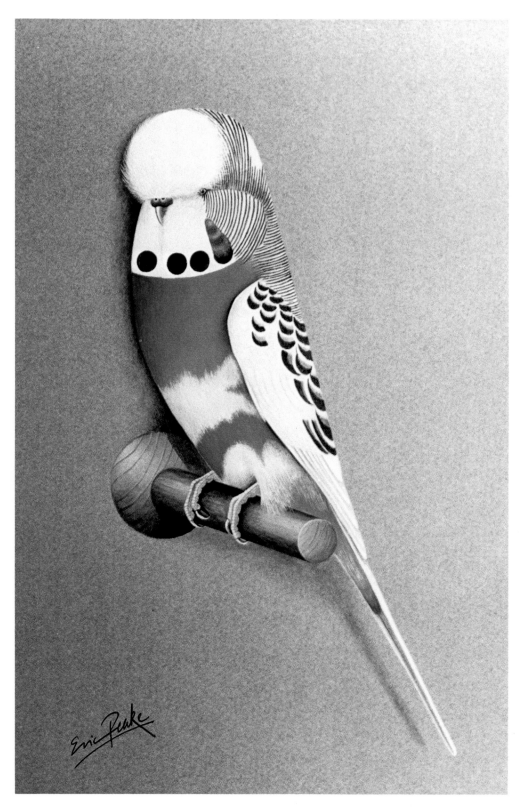

Plate 20. Dominant Blue Pied (Modern Type)

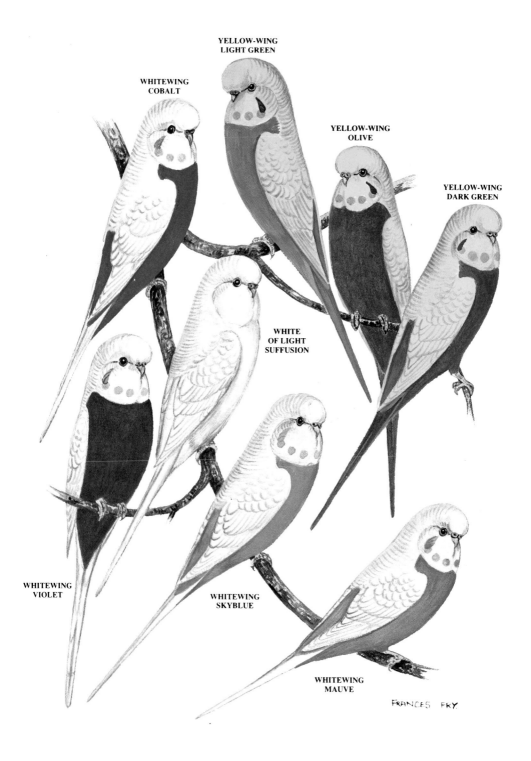

**WHITEWING
COBALT**

**YELLOW-WING
LIGHT GREEN**

**YELLOW-WING
OLIVE**

**YELLOW-WING
DARK GREEN**

**WHITE
OF LIGHT
SUFFUSION**

**WHITEWING
VIOLET**

**WHITEWING
SKYBLUE**

**WHITEWING
MAUVE**

FRANCES FRY

Plate 21. Various Colours of Budgerigars I.

GREYWING
LIGHT GREEN

ALBINO

FALLOW
LIGHT GREEN

LUTINO

YELLOW-
FACED
SKYBLUE

GREYWING
SKYBLUE

FALLOW
SKYBLUE

FRANCES FRY

*Note addition of cheek fleck in Lutino — this is shown in ''The Budgerigar Book''
and other reference books.

Plate 22.   Various Colours of Budgerigars II

OPALINE
GREY GREEN

OPALINE
SKYBLUE

OPALINE
LIGHT GREEN

OPALINE
DARK
GREEN

OPALINE
COBALT

OPALINE
MAUVE

OPALINE
VIOLET

OPALINE
GREY

FRANCES FRY

Plate 23. Various Colours of Budgerigars III

A.

B.

Plate 24

A. Australian Spangles first bred in Europe in 1980.
   Sky Blue, Light Green, and Yellow Faced Sky-Blue.

B. Opaline Sky Blue and Mauve.

THE APPROVED SCALE OF POINTS

	Size.	Shape of Body.	Carriage.	Head.	Colour.	Mask.	Wing Markings.	Quality of Feather.
LIGHT GREEN	10	20	10	20	20	10	7	3
DARK GREEN	10	20	10	20	20	10	7	3
OLIVE GREEN	10	20	10	20	20	10	7	3
LIGHT YELLOW	10	20	10	20	37	—	—	3
DARK YELLOW	10	20	10	20	37	—	—	3
OLIVE YELLOW	10	20	10	20	37	—	—	3
COBALT	10	20	10	20	20	10	7	3
SKYBLUE	10	20	10	20	20	10	7	3
MAUVE	10	20	10	20	20	10	7	3
WHITE BLUE, COBALT, or MAUVE (Light suffusion)	10	20	10	20	37	—	—	3
WHITE, BLUE, COBALT, or MAUVE (Dark suffusion)	10	20	10	20	30	—	7*	3
GREYWING LIGHT GREEN	10	20	10	20	17	8	12	3
GREYWING DARK GREEN	10	20	10	20	17	8	12	3
GREYWING OLIVE GREEN	10	20	10	20	17	8	12	3
GREYWING SKYBLUE	10	20	10	20	17	8	12	3
GREYWING COBALT	10	20	10	20	17	8	12	3
GREYWING MAUVE	10	20	10	20	17	8	12	3
CINNAMONWING LIGHT GREEN	10	20	10	20	17	8	12	3
CINNAMONWING DARK GREEN	10	20	10	20	17	8	12	3
CINNAMONWING OLIVE	10	20	10	20	17	8	12	3
CINNAMONWING SKYBLUE	10	20	10	20	17	8	12	3
CINNAMONWING COBALT	10	20	10	20	17	8	12	3
CINNAMONWING MAUVE	10	20	10	20	17	8	12	3
FALLOW LIGHT GREEN	10	20	10	20	17	10	10	3
FALLOW DARK GREEN	10	20	10	20	17	10	10	3
FALLOW OLIVE GREEN	10	20	10	20	17	10	10	3
FALLOW SKY BLUE	10	20	10	20	17	10	10	3
FALLOW COBALT	10	20	10	20	17	10	10	3
FALLOW MAUVE	10	20	10	20	17	10	10	3
CLEAR YELLOW, RED EYE	10	20	10	20	37	—	—	3
CLEAR WHITE RED EYE	10	20	10	20	37	—	—	3

Note: This Schedule applies only to birds that are in condition. Birds that are not fit, or have definite faults such as claws, flight or tail feathers missing, spots down, etc., must be handicapped in proportion to their failings.

* The 7 points allotted to wing marking in Whites of Dark Suffusion are for *absence* of wing markings, not presence of wing markings as in the case of the other colours.

23

much pleasure in acceding to our request. I thereupon wrote to a member of the King's household asking him 'to convey to the King the Society's most grateful and dutiful thanks for the high honour His Majesty has bestowed on us, and an expression of our loyalty and devotion to our Royal Patron." These sentiments I know will be endorsed by every member. We trust that the Budgerigars in the Royal Aviaries at Sandringham will prosper and afford great pleasure to His Majesty.

The Club's Title

We understand that it was the wish of His Majesty the King that our club should be called 'The Budgerigar Society', rather than by its present title.

In conformity with this the change is now being made, and we shall henceforth be known as 'The Budgerigar Society'.

H.S. Stokes.

His Majesty King George V was patron until his sad death, and the Society benefited greatly from his support and his interest in breeding Budgerigars.

COLOUR MUTATIONS

In 1925, when the **Budgerigar Club (Society)** was inaugurated, 116 members were enrolled and some six years later, in 1930, only 59 of these were still members, although the Society had grown significantly in strength. There can be little doubt whatsoever that one of the great contributing factors to the rise of the Budgerigar from the status of an interesting little Parrakeet to being an exceedingly popular world-wide household pet, aviary, breeding and exhibition bird, is its amazing tendency to mutate. The first significant break in colour, apart from the Yellow, was the Blue form; this was originally bred in Belgium in 1881, but it was not until 1910 that it was seen in Great Britain and then it created a great stir in our cage and aviary bird world.

The development of the domesticated Budgerigar was progressing very rapidly up to the first world war, when there was a shut down on the extension of breeding of all birds, both at home and overseas. It is said that at the onset of hostilities the famous French commercial breeders, Bastide Brothers, were forced to kill more than 100,000 Budgerigars.

During the war years however a further far reaching mutation, the Dark or Satin Green, occurred in the commercial aviaries of Blanchard of Toulouse, France. The appearance of the Dark Green mutation eventually led to the production of Olive Green, Cobalt and Mauve shades. There is a most enlightening article by J. Bailly-Maitre on Budgerigar breeding in France at that time in the *Avicultural Magazine* of October 1925, together with a colour plate of seven colours. (For the details of this colour phase the reader should turn to the pages dealing with the individual colours.) In the early twenties, when the world began to settle down to a more peaceful state, the breeding of Budgerigars

Figure 2.5   Blue Cock. Winner at Crystal Palace 1930

Figure 2.6   A Talking Budgerigar owned and trained by C. R. Phillips of Lakemba near Sydney in the 1930's.

started another era of development.

One area of development, was in the teaching of Budgerigars to talk. Since Dr. Russ's report on this subject numbers of birds in various countries had been trained, but this accomplishment was not widely known to the public until W.R.H. Bearby of West Hartlepool, gave a graphic description of his talking Bird in the *Budgerigar Bulletin* No. 3 of December 1927. This knowledge was a further help in the development of the Budgerigar as a desirable domesticated bird.

By this time new colour mutations were appearing in rapid succession in different parts of the world, which encouraged scientifically minded bird lovers to begin investigating the hereditary behaviour of these new forms. Foremost amongst the early investigators were Dr. Hans Duncker and Konsul General Carl H. Cremer of Bremen, Germany. These two eminent ornithologists applies *Mendel's Theory of Inheritance* to Budgerigar colour breeding and carried out many hundreds of strictly controlled cross pairings.

Mendel's Theory of Inheritance

A note is perhaps needed to explain the relevance of Mendel's theory. Gregor Mendel was a Monk, living in Austria over 100 years ago, who

Figure 2.7 Gregor Mendel, the pioneer of inheritance theory.

27

started experimenting with the crossing of different strains of peas and other forms of garden vegetables. He accumulated a mass of records and it became clear from his crossing and re-crossing of the plants that the results formed definite and consistent patterns. He published his first scientific observations during the year 1866, but they did not appear to make any impression on other scientific observers of that period. At the beginning of this century Professor DeVries of Amsterdam, Holland, reviewed Mendel's old writings and realised the significance of his discovery. Shortly after this, in 1905, Professor W. Bateson of Cambridge University published a book entitled *Mendel's Principles of Heredity*, thereby making this valuable information available to all plant and animal breeders. This book was just preceded by one from Professor R.C. Punnett, also of Cambridge University, entitled *Mendelism*, which gave details of Mendel's enlightening theory. In 1911 A.D. Darbishire, M.A., of London and Edinburgh Universities wrote an explanatory book on *Breeding and the Mendelian Discovery* giving details of Mendel's Laws as applied to both plants and animals, including poultry. No mention was made of these Laws applying to other birds and it was not until Dr. H. Duncker of Bremen, Germany, realised the vast possibilities of the theory and applied them to Budgerigars that they were

Figure 2.8 Professor Bateson, who translated Mendel's work into English.

universally adopted for bird breeding.

Duncker and Cremer, applying Mendel's laws to their pairings, proved beyond all doubt that each of the different colour mutations operated in their own particular way and thus cross pairing results could be calculated accurately. In due course the *Book of Budgerigar Colour Expectations* was published, in 1932, deriving from information on matings published in earlier *Bulletins of The Budgerigar Society* and became the guide to colour breeders all over the world. I had the honour and pleasure of testing and collating many of the early Greywing breeding results and eventually checking all the mating calculations in the *Book of Budgerigar Colour Expectations*, so ably translated from the German by the late F.S. Elliott of Ipswich the then Editor of the *Budgerigar Bulletin*. This book went into a considerable number of editions and contained some 1860 expectation calculations of colour crosses. There was also good explanatory coverage of the new mutations that were not included in the calculated expectations. Unfortunately this very valuable book went out of print many years ago and it has not been possible for the **Budgerigar Society** to reprint because of the vast capital outlay. Old copies can still be found at times in shops that deal with ornithological literature.

Before the publication of the book of *Colour Expectations* the validity of the Mendel theory, as applied to Budgerigars by Dr. Hans Duncker, was discussed at great length by believers and non-believers in the Fancy Press, the *Budgerigar Society Bulletin* and whenever Budgerigar enthusiasts met. Two of the chief opponents of the Mendel theory were J. Bradshaw and J.W. Marsden, both really experienced and enthusiastic Budgerigar breeders. Their difference with the Mendel theory in fact was quite small and was summed up exceedingly well in a pamphlet published by General Consul Carl Cremer in January of 1928:

> The difference is quite small, Mr. Marsden holds on to 'pedigree and hereditary' whereas Mendelism is interested in pedigree only so far as existing hereditary factors have been influenced by ancestors. I cannot help stating again that our experiments have not delivered any proof in favour of a long line of ancestry.

MUTATION DEVELOPMENTS

During the period when the many colour mutations were occurring and being developed, the *Any Other Colour* classes at many exhibitions contained considerable numbers of colourful and interesting exhibits and were a centre of attraction to fanciers. The Fancy Press, Societies' magazines, and ornithological literature poured forth a wealth of information and facts supported by controlled breeding results to the great benefit of all Budgerigar breeders. The period of mutation developments, the 1930's, was, indeed, a wonderfully peaceful, yet extremely competitive time both for breeders and exhibitors and can well be considered as the golden age of the Budgerigar Fancy.

A further impetus to Budgerigar keeping and breeding was given by Beauty Medcalf, a very talented talking Budgerigar, featured on Radio on February 28th 1938. An excellent report of this broadcast was quoted by W. Watmough in *Budgerigar Bulletin* No. 45 of March 1938. The history of this famous talking bird was given by Percy G. Frudd in his book *Incomparable Budgerigars* published in 1938. From that time onwards tame single talking Budgerigars have become the favourite household pet birds all over the world.

Many keen breeders have had their first introduction to Budgerigars by possessing a tame Budgerigar in their youth. Tame talking Budgerigars have given and continue to give untold pleasure and compansionship to the aged, handicapped and housebound people of all ages.

EARLY EXHIBITORS

Amongst the earlier exhibitors were Mrs. D. Wall, R.J. Watts, Denys Weston, Allen Silver, H. Tod Boyd, Tom Goodwin, Andrew Wilson, M.T. Allen, C.H. Rogers, H.C. Humphries, Cyril Whale and Edwin North, to name a few. In the following decade some of these names became less prominent on the show bench and others, such as Mrs. E. Watmough, Mrs. E.K. Goddard, Miss Vera Scott, Walter Higham, N.H. Danby. F.W. Gavey, S. Hodgson, R.E. Hyde, H. Bryan, J. Landsburgh, W.A. Fitch, Arthur Collier, Frank Wait for example, began to appear in the lists of successful exhibitors. The efforts of these keen fanciers did much to popularise both the new and the older colours, and Budgerigars generally throughout the country.

Domesticated Exhibition Type

The birds being exhibited during this period were becoming rather different in type and substance to those seen during the early part of the Budgerigar Society's show events. It would seem that breeders were steadily evolving a domesticated exhibition type that was markedly different in many respects from the smaller round headed wild type. The head was becoming bolder, the mask deeper, the throat spots larger and overall it was of more substantial build. These changes were mainly to be found amongst the normal colours with the fast appearing new colours very steadily catching up, through the perseverance of their enthusiastic breeders. Generally it took a considerable time for some of the newer colours to reach the perfection of the Normals, as most of these

30

new colours had occurred in uncontrolled breeding stocks and were naturally of the older wild type.

World War II Period

Up to the beginning of World War II Budgerigars had developed considerably and were being bred in most countries in the world. British bred Budgerigars were considered to be the best and our stock was exported far and wide. The Ideal Budgerigar as depicted in *Budgerigar Bulletin* No. 44 of December 1937 together with the scale of points (see pages 22–3) was in operation until a new Ideal was brought into being some decades later. The global disruption created by World War II caused the Budgerigar, and in fact all bird breeding, to be virtually suspended. Nevertheless, small pockets of Budgerigars were maintained under great difficulties by dedicated people, so that when peace came there was a nucleus of most colours from which to build up the fancy once again.

The 1940's and 50's

In the late 1940's and 1950's Budgerigar keeping, breeding and exhibiting revived at an amazing rate and quite a boom in Budgerigars developed. The trend in numbers and colours of birds exhibited shows quite clearly in the figures given below for the **National (Red Cross) Exhibition** in November 1945:

Champion Adult Section:

21 Light Green Cocks, 19 Light Yellow cocks and hens, 7 Greywing cocks and hens, 20 Opaline cocks and hens and 22 Any Other Colour cocks and hens.

Young Bird Classes:

36 Light Green cocks, 22 Light Yellow cocks and hens, 16 Opaline cocks and hens and 23 Any Other Colour cocks and hens.

It is interesting to note that there were only seven adult Greywings and no young birds. The largest class in the other Sections was the Novice Light Green cocks with twenty-seven.

In 1951, the entries at that year's **National Exhibition** indicated that Budgerigars were really making their mark as exhibition birds:

Champion Adults:

49 Light Green cocks, 32 hens, 22 Light Yellow cocks and hens, 41 Grey and Grey Green cocks and hens, 49 Lutino cocks, 31 hens, and 20 Any Other Colour cocks and hens.

Young Birds:

52 Light Green cocks, 51 hens, 23 Light Yellow cocks and hens, 63 Grey or Grey Green cocks and hens, 34 Lutino cocks and 23 hens and 52 Sky Blue cocks.

Novice Adults:
52 Light Green cocks and 25 hens, 31 Grey or Grey Green cocks and hens, 34 Lutino cocks and 15 hens.

Novice Young Bird Section:
41 Light Green cocks and 32 hens, 48 Sky Blue cocks and hens, 33 Lutino cocks and hens and 25 Any Other Colour cocks and hens.

At the following year's Event the classes just mentioned had some 30% increase in entries excluding Light Yellows which seemed on the decline, Greywings were now being shown together with Cinnamons which made up most of the entries in these mixed classes, Opalines were increasing in popularity and numbers and the Visual Violets had a class of their own and drew no less than forty entries. These limited figures give some indication as to the tremendous development of the Budgerigar in the cage bird world.

Budgerigar Society Membership

The membership of the **Budgerigar Society** ran into many thousands and all the Area Societies had very big increases in their membership. Local Societies catering solely for Budgerigars sprang into being and there were Budgerigar shows staged up and down the country. The Budgerigar classifications at many big cage bird exhibitions were greatly extended and these classes were invariably extremely well supported. A new Ideal Budgerigar was approved by the **Budgerigar Society** during this period of development and in general the overall quality of Budgerigars steadily improved.

Importation

The ban on the importing of Parrot-like birds which included Budgerigars had been in force since before the War because of a Psittacosis scare and was lifted in 1952 for a period. During this time considerable numbers of Budgerigars were imported into this country from Europe, mainly to satisfy the vastly increased pet bird trade. Although these Continental birds were mostly not of such good exhibition quality as our home produced stock they did supply new 'blood' to Budgerigar stocks. Except for the small quantity of birds especially imported under licence it had been many years since fresh stock had been freely available to the Fancy.

Feed

From the period from about 1940 to the middle of the fifties bird seed had used all kinds of other food to supplement the usual canary and millet seeds. Fortunately a seed called *Persicaria* did much to keep Budgerigars in a fit healthy condition as it was freely available at a reasonable price. For instance, in the 1949/50 season the price of canary seed ranged from £8-£12, white millet £20-£24, yellow millet £17-£20 per cwt, whereas *Persicaria* was about £3-£4 per cwt, quite a difference. This sample of seed prices is most revealing when compared with those ruling at the present time; also it is interesting to note that Budgerigars thrived and bred well when fed mainly on *Persicaria* for quite a long period.

FRENCH MOULT

Whilst Budgerigars were being fed to a great extent on foods other than canary and millet seeds, the instances of French Moult reported amongst breeding stocks were very low and limited. French Moult did not appear in Great Britain as a real scourge until extensive breeding, together with inbreeding mainly in cages had been practised for some years. The first investigation in this country into French Moult was carried out by the late Dr. M.D.S. Armour and his findings appeared in a supplement to the March 1936 No. 37 issue of **The Budgerigar Bulletin**. His controlled experiments covered several years and embraced many breeding results, and his conclusion was that French Moult was hereditary. This opinion is well explained in a foreword to the supplement contributed by Professor F.A.E. Crew, M.D., D.Sc.,

Figure 2.9 Persicaria (*Polygonum Persicaria*).

33

Ph.D., then Director of Animal Genetics, Edinburgh. Professor Crew who writes:

Dear Dr. Armour,

I have read your article on French Moult and think it a most valuable piece of work. You produce the straightforward experimental evidence one has looked for, and I sincerely hope your conclusions will be accepted by Budgerigar breeders and your advice as to the only method of eradicating the disease followed.

To come down to particular points: I should say that there seems to be no reason to suppose that French Moult is due to the operation of more than one recessive factor; a wide variation of expression may be due as much to environmental causes as to genetic modifying factors; but obviously there is a single gene which is responsible for the presence or absence of the disease. Genes that modify the expression of the disease, if these exist, would be dependent for their effect on the presence of the gene for French Moult, and, in its absence, are probably harmless in themselves.

It is interesting that your set of experiments has proved the genetic nature not only of French Moult, but also of feather plucking and of bad feeding — two aspects of Budgerigar morality which might be followed up and related genetically with the colour factors.

About the connection between the deficiency of blue and the presence of French Moult, I do not think there is necessarily any genetic basis. I should regard the colour deficiency as an accidental or secondary effect of the faulty feather structure, not in any way connected with the colour factors.

F.A.E. Crew.

Dr. Armour's findings were similar to those of Dr. H. Steiner of Zürich which had been published in *Budgerigar Bulletins*. Several other theories had been advanced in *Budgerigar Bulletins, Cage Birds* and other Journals, all of which fitted in with certain aspects of French Moult but none covered the whole. In spite of all the advice presented, French Moult continued to flourish amongst breeding stocks of all colours.

In 1956 an investigation was mounted by the National Council of Aviculture in a determined effort to try and discover the cause of French Moult and if possible a cure. Reading University was chosen for the project and Professor C. Tyler, B.Sc., Ph.D., F.R.I.C., was in general supervision with Dr. (now Professor) T.G. Taylor directing the work, assisted by Mrs. P.M. Tindal. After extensive experiments had been conducted under ideal conditions no firm answer to the question was found, but it did seem from the evidence that hereditary, feeding and environmental conditions all played a part. It was found however that an excess of vitamin A could accelerate the French Moult condition. Having examined all the available evidence about French Moult published over many years and, together with some experiments and findings of my own, I am firmly of the opinion that French Moult can only be eradicated from Budgerigar stocks by stopping the use of any known tainted birds in the breeding quarters.

THE BUDGERIGAR SOCIETY STANDARD SHOW CAGE

The implementation period to be 10 years with effect from the 1996 Show Season.

Standard Show Cage Specification

SIZE Overall measurements 355mm long x 305mm high x 165mm wide.

BOTTOM   355mm long x 162mm wide x 6mm thick with pencil round front edge. Maker's code number to be indented on the base of cage so that in no way visible when judging takes place.

SIDES   293mm high x 162mm wide x 9mm thick with pencil round front edge and 251mm radius in top front corner.

TOP 355mm long x 140mm wide x 6mm thick with pencil round front edge and 85mm x 30mm kidney shaped hand hold position centrally in length and 40mm from rear.

BACK 355mm long x 230mm high x 3mm thick.

SLOPING ROOF 9mm thick positioned 222mm from bottom of cage and 45mm from front of cage. Centre of junction between top of cage and sloping roof to be stiffened by a triangular block of wood.

FRONT RAIL 70mm high from floor of cage x 9mm thick and recessed 4mm from front of cage. Registered Trade Mark label to be fitted to front rail set in bottom left hand corner with No. 2 $^{3/8}$ slotted round head brass screws.

DOOR SIZE   100mm high x 90mm wide externally with sloping bevel cut to top, bottom and left hand edges. Right hand edge to be straight cut. Bottom of door to be 95mm from bottom of cage and centred on side panel. Door corners an the opposite side to the hinges can be radiused up to 5mm.

DOOR FASTENERS 1.   One plain brass desk turn 25mm long fixed by brass screw to side of cage to coincide with a raised head brass screw positioned 12mm in from front left hand edge of door and 50mm from top of door.

2. One plain brass desk turn 25mm long fixed above top left hand side of door to line up with side fixing set 12mm from edge of door.

DOOR HINGES Two black painted strong hinges 25mm x 16mm fixed on right hand side of door and I0mm from top and bottom of door. **DOOR PULL** 18/25mm x 1.6mm (16 gauge) wire, black painted, S hook in centre of door.

PERCH SIZE 14/15mm diameter with both ends cut flush. **PERCH POSITION** Centre of perches and screw holes to be 140mm from bottom of cage and 112mm apart.

PERCH FIXINGS Perches to be secured to back of cage with counter sunk screws and brass cup washers and to centre crossbar on wire front of cage by 3mm deep horizontal saw cut.

WIRE FRONT Comprises of 21 wires x 2mm (14 gauge) mesh at 16mm centres. For strength, double punched set 10mm apart; curve at top, 19mm bow. Centre of middle crossbar to be 140mm above bottom of cage. Front to be fixed to cage by three extended wires at bottom and top. The centre wire at top of the cage to be cut to avoid excessive protrusion.

DRINKERS White plastic finger drawer type not to exceed 50mm in length and should be placed between the 3rd and 4th wire from left and resting on the middle bar at all times.

COLOURS Inside and wire front – White. Outside Black gloss, including top of front rail.

Preferred material for making cages is red or white deal, pine or obeche with the top and bottom a 6mm finish and the sides and false roof a 9mm finish. The back a 3mm plywood nailed outside. However cages produced in alternative materials must comply wiih all internal and external dimensions and give a similar appearance to a wooden cage when viewed from the front.

STANDARD SHOW CAGE
incorporating BS Patent No. 755106

Figure 2.10 Modern Standard Show Cage
Details kindly supplied by The Budgerigar Society

● ●

THE SCALE OF POINTS

The scale of points gives guidance to judges and fanciers on the value attached to the specified features of a bird. For the perfect bird it will be seen that *Size, shape, balance and deportment* are given 35 points and the **Head, etc,** is given 25 points. This means that 60 points go to what is loosely called **'Type'**.

Colour is 15 points for many of the varieties, but 40 points are awarded to those which require *depth of colour,* eg, Lutino, Dark Eyed (clears) and Yellows. Other variations exist for *crested birds* and for *contrast of colour or variegation.*

36

THE BUDGERIGAR SOCIETY'S
SCALE OF POINTS

Variety	Size shape balance and deportment	Size & shape of head incl. mask & where applicable spots	Colour	Variety markings
Normal (Light, Dark, Olive, Grey Green)	35	25	15	25
Normal (Skyblue, Cobalt, Mauve, Violet, Grey)	35	25	15	25
Opaline (Light, Dark, Olive, Grey Green)	35	25	15	25
Opaline (Skyblue, Cobalt, Mauve, Violet, Grey)	35	25	15	25
Cinnamon (Light, Dark, Olive, Grey Green)	35	25	15	25
Cinnamon (Skyblue, Cobalt, Mauve, Violet & Grey)	35	25	15	25
Opaline Cinnamon (Light, Dark, Olive, Grey Green)	35	25	15	25
Opaline Cinnamon (Skyblue, Cobalt, Mauve, Violet, Grey)	35	25	15	25
Lutino & Albino	35	25	40*	–
Clearwings (Yellow-wings & Whitewings Light, Dark, Olive & Grey Green Skyblue, Cobalt, Mauve, Violet & Grey)	35	25	15	25
Crested or Tufted (in all shades & varieties)	35	25	15	25+
Spangles (in all shades & varieties)	35	25	15	25
Spangles Double Factor	35	25	40*	–
Pied (Dominant) (in all shades & all varieties)	35	25	15	25
Pied (Clearflighted) (in all shades & all varieties)	35	25	15	25
Pied (Recessive) (in all shades & all varieties)	35	25	15	25#
Dark-Eyed (Clear Varieties)	35	25	40*	–
Yellowface (Mutant 1, Mutant 2 and Goldenface all varieties Blue Series)	35	25	15	25
Rainbows (Opaline Whitewing Yellowface & Goldenface)	35	25	15	25
Yellow (Light, Dark, Olive) (including Opaline & Cinnamon)	35	25	40*	–
Yellow & White (Suffused) (in all shades including Opaline & Cinnamon)	35	25	15	25
Grey Yellow & Grey White (in all shades (light, medium & dark) incl Opaline & Cinnamon)	35	25	15	25
Greywing (Light, Dark, Olive, Grey Green, Skyblue, Cobalt, Mauve, Violet & Grey) (including Opaline Greywing)	35	25	15	25
Lacewings (Yellow & White) (incl. Opalines)	35	25	15	25
Fallow (Light, Dark, Olive, Grey Green, Skyblue, Cobalt, Mauve, Violet & Grey) (including Opaline Fallow)	35	25	15	25
Opaline, Cinnamon & Opal. Cin. Clearwings	35	25	15	25

* Points for depth and clarity of colour
# Points for contrast of colour and variegation and % of wing markings
+ Points included for shape and quality of Crest

Team of six birds of any colour or team of four of any one colour.
Points: General colour & variety 50; uniformity 50.

MODERN COLOUR DEVELOPMENTS

As shown in the preceding pages, the colours bred in captivity and their many variations, are far removed from the original green budgerigar introduced to the world by John Gould. The Budgerigar Society and its members have been responsible for the mammoth task of recording the standards and full details can be obtained from their office in Northampton or in one of the standard works on Budgerigars*.

In recent times the standard colours have been painted by Eric Peake the renowned bird artist and what a difference this has made for the fancier who has had difficulty in determining what a particular variety looks like. This process started in 1980 and has been extended from that time.**

One of the main differences seen in the 20 years or so since the first painting has been the change in the head and its parts. The cap and brow have changed thus improving the appearance of the head.

Birds have become more "streamlined" and the flights are quite rounded. However, the birds are still quite balanced which is an important requirement.

The question of TYPE and COLOUR is always controversial, but it is generally agreed that both aspects must be considered when a bird is being judged. A top class colour on a badly shaped bird is of little value and this principle needs to be applied at all times. The modern approach recognizes this important fact.

---

* For example *The Cult of the Budgerigar*, W Watmough, revised by James Blake.

** See *The New Ideal Budgerigar* an article by Roy Stringer and Eric Peake, which appears in *Cage & Aviary Birds* magazine, 6th November, 2000.

CHAPTER 3

HISTORY OF THE MUTATIONS
I — THE EARLY COLOURS

When John Gould first brought wild Green Budgerigars to Europe and they began to breed quite freely, their owners had no idea how, in due course, a fantastic range of colour mutations would occur. From all published records, it would seem beyond any doubt that yellow was the first break in the colour of Budgerigars. After Light Greens had been breeding perfectly true to colour for some thirty odd years it was in 1871/72 that Yellows were first reported to have been bred in Belgium.

YELLOWS

In his notes, L. van der Snickt (Belgium) records having seen a Yellow pair in 1872 in a large batch of Greens. Unfortunately these Yellows and their parents were killed without leaving any progeny. It was not until some five years later, in 1877, when van der Snickt again saw Yellows, and this time there were some fourteen examples in a flight containing fifty pairs. He stated that they were not all clear Yellows (**Lutinos**), some having a greenish suffusion on their chests and underparts (**suffused Yellows**). This difference in colour points strongly to the fact that the clear ones were Lutinos and the suffused ones were the ordinary common suffused Yellows. This indicated that both normal-eyed and red-eyed Yellows were in existence at the same period, and that the birds van der Snickt saw were collected from various sources.

A further Yellow form is also mentioned, which would appear to be the forerunner of the exhibition Light Yellow or **Buttercup Yellow**. It seems that the original clear Yellows (Lutinos) were all hens, as would be expected nowadays, and through lack of genetical knowledge they were not established at that particular time. The other two normal-eyed forms of Yellows were undoubtedly the ancestors of the ordinary

39

suffused Yellows and the exhibition Yellows. The different shades of yellow, Lutinos excluded, are due to the same, or a series of the same chromosome changes as they give only Yellow birds when paired together. The actual variation in purity of colour can be brought about by selective breeding and the presence or absence of modifying agents.

In the *Budgerigar Bulletin* No. 17 of June 1931 the late Allen Silver stated:

> **Among wild birds (Budgerigars) and skins of wild birds there is no reference to white or blue birds. The Keartland reference to a yellow bird being seen in a wild flock on three occasions and the J.P. Roger's account in Emu Volume II p.62 of 1902, stating that a specimen 'Of a decided yellow colour' are the only records with which I am familiar.**

These statements indicate that Yellows had actually appeared and had been seen in the wild flocks, and as recessives would quickly have been absorbed by the dominant natural green colour should they have bred. We know that when **Light Yellow** is crossed with **Light Green** all the resulting chicks are **green** in colour and carry the yellow character hidden in their genetical make-up. It is therefore possible that one or more of the early imported Australian Light Greens could have been a yellow carrier. If such a bird happens to be in a flock of Greens breeding together in an aviary for a number of years, it is always possible that two yellow carrying Greens would mate together and produce Yellow young. This possibility has not been put forward previously and the early Yellows have all been thought of as being due to a mutation in captivity. This may well have been the case with the early Yellows, but the possibility of a Yellow carrier being imported should also be borne in mind.

As it has been shown, **Lutinos,** clear Yellows with red eyes, were appearing in the 1870's and 1880's, but the strains had not been in existence for very long and it was a great many years before free breeding strains of Lutinos and Albinos were evolved in Germany and other countries.

Dr. Karl Russ (Germany) writes in about 1879 that he saw a yellow hen with a **dark green** feather on its breast and almost black undulations on its wings. If this description is accurate and the feather on the breast was actually dark green then the bird must have been the first to have a dark character in its genetical make-up. It was not until 1915 that Blanchard Bros. (France) are reported as having produced Dark Green (Laurel Green) Budgerigars. Two other Yellows with black undulations were seen by Dr. Karl Russ during the 1880's, one in the aviaries of M. Kessels (Uccle, Belgium) and the other as a preserved skin. It is not known if these **black marked Yellows** ever produced young as

40

nothing more seems to have been heard of them. Since that time similarly marked Yellows have been reported as appearing both in British and European aviaries but did not reproduce their like.

In 1884 Mr. Joseph Abrahams, London, is said to have bred the first Yellows in Great Britain from Yellow parent birds brought over from Belgium. Some two years later, birds of the same Yellow strain were exhibited at a show in London for the first time by W. Swaysland. From then onwards to the first decade of the present century Yellows were being bred in a number of European aviaries and were also bred and exhibited in small numbers in Great Britain. In the few years prior to World War I some bird breeders in Great Britain were beginning to specialise in the production of **Light Yellow** Budgerigars and improving and enriching their colour using as stock, selected birds mostly of European origin. From amongst those early Light Yellow specialists the name of R.J. Watts stands out clearly as it was mainly through his unfailing interest and efforts that Light Yellows made their spectacular progress as exhibition birds in this country.

Early Exhibitors

The following extract from Allen Silver's series *A Monograph on Budgerigars and their Culture* No. 13 which appeared in *The Budgerigar Bulletin* No. 29 of March 1934 throws considerable light on early Budgerigar exhibitors and judges:

In our early teens)1894) we looked forward to their return from the Crystal Palace shows of those days, in order to hear about the exhibits and peruse the catalogue. For a period of over thirty years I have, almost without a break, been present at these events and, whilst engaged in compiling a list of birds, which had appeared on the benches of our shows, some twenty years ago, I particularly noticed the dearth of interest shown regarding the Budgerigar as a show bird and also how the amalgamation of its class with other species had brought about an almost total extinction of entries and interest. Two years previous to the War a mild interest arose and a class was provided for 'Greens' at the Horticultural Hall, London, in 1913; also at one or two shows in the provinces a Budgerigar class was given. At the Horticultural Hall Show seventeen entries turned up and the first prize was won by Dan Longden of Swansea (a well known cage bird exhibitor in his day) . . . About this period enthusiasts regarding the exhibition merits of Budgerigars could be numbered on one's hands but a very friendly and intimate competition arose amongst such people as Miss A.B. Smyth, Mrs. Bayly Ransom, Messrs. J. Frostick, B. Longden, A.J. Shipton, R.J. Watts and myself, all associated with the Foreign Bird Exhibitors' League of that day . . . After the cessation of hostilities the threads were slowly but gradually picked up although entries were small; but a new interest was awakening. A class for Budgerigars was provided at the Olympia Shows of 1922 and 1923 and in 1924 the Dulwich and Peckham Cage Bird Society promoted the first post war Crystal Palace Bird Show, giving a class for Greens and Yellows which contained ten entries.

In reviewing the decade between 1873-83 we find amongst exhibitors the names of Miss Hawkins (a daughter of the famed Hawkins of Bear Street, London) Groom, Sumner, Judd, Otty, Dr. T.W. Greene, and Newmarch (a forerunner of the present manager of Gamages Zoo Department). The judges were such people as Harrison Weir (the bird and animal artist), John Jenner Weir (his brother) and probably Major Howarth Ashton. The classes were mostly headed Australian Grass Parrakeets (in pairs) and in 1877 owners commenced describing their exhibits as 'Budgerigars' and the classes contained very few entries, numbering as low as four, but usually between five and thirteen, although in 1879 twenty-nine entires were benched and in 1883 twenty-two.

Between 1884 and 1889 the names of J. Frostick, C.P. Arthur, Walter Swaysland, J. Dewar, C.T. Maxwell, H.J. Fulljames, R.T. Storey and Cronkshaw appeared in the classes for Budgerigars. Foreign bird judges who judged such classes for the period were the Hon. Canon Button, Dr. C. Simpson, J. Abrahams, H.T. Camps and the Rev. H.D. Astley; all names inseparable from the annals of aviculture. At this period we note Walter Swaysland showing 'Yellows' and in 1902 we find an entry of seven Budgerigars with Swaysland judging. Amalgamation of the Budgerigar class with Lovebirds and Hanging Parrots in 1903 and subsequently until 1913, practically excluded them (Budgerigars) from the show bench. Charles Cooper of Brixton persisted in showing a few against great odds and occasionally won and the principal Parrot judge acting at this period was H.T. Camps of Ely, Cambs.

In the following year, 1925, the **Budgerigar Club** was formed at the Crystal Palace Show and Budgerigars were entered for competition in two classes consisting of seventeen birds. Most of the names mentioned in the above extract have long since passed from the memories of fanciers but it should always be remembered that it was through their persistent efforts that started Budgerigars on their progression to international fame.

THE BLUE PHASE

Although there has been a galaxy of wonderful colour changes in the plumage of the Budgerigar, the admiration and amazement created by the appearance of the Blue phase has probably never been equalled. The following extract from the *Avicultural Magazine*, Vol. III, No. 10, of Ocober 1925, indicates how this colour was introduced to aviculture. J. Bailly Mattre of France writes:

A coloured plate, whch was published in 1882 by l'Acclimatation Illustres' of Brussels, Belgium, enables us to form an exact idea of the new coloured plumage in which this variety was first clad. The pair which figured there differ little from the type which we see now among more or less azure blue specimens. The birds which served as models for this plate belonged to M. Limbock of Uccle, Belgium, who preserved the strain with jealous care.

It was not until some thirty years later to our knowledge, that the Blue Budgerigar was introduced into France; and in any case it was not until February 1911, that it was publicly shown in Paris by Mme. Quentin de la Gueriniers. (The first Blue Budgerigar displayed in the Natural History Museum was offered that year by Mme. de la Gueriniere and presented to our colleagues of the Societe d'Acclimatation at the sitting of the 4th December, 1911, by Professor Huessart). It is superfluous to say that they were considered exquisite, seeing that nowadays every amateur has the opportunity of admiring this variety.

It will be seen from the following further extract from Allen Silver's Monograph in *Budgerigar Bulletin* No. 19 of December 1931 that Blue Budgerigars were first exhibited and seen in Great Britain in 1910:

Eighteen eighty one seems to have been the year associated with the first appearance of the Blue birds. The birds of M. Limbosch of Uccle serving as models to a plate, (see previous extract from *Avicultural Magazine* **Vol. III No. 10) also the** *Budgerigar* **by Dr. Karl Russ. The van der Snickt report 1881 mentions that the first bird was a male and was paired to a Yellow female and their young were all yellow. Later in 1881 a female Blue was obtained from the same pair which produced the first Blue male. This hen was blue all over her body but her tail and head were yellow. Unfortunately the two blue birds were not paired; the female is now brooding with a yellow male.**

If van der Snickt is correct in his descriptions of the birds and the breeding result from the Blue cock it raises some extremely interesting possibilities. He writes that the Blue cock when paired to a Yellow hen gave all Yellow young. In the light of present day knowledge of Budgerigar genetics we know that a pure Blue paired to a pure Yellow will give only green coloured young. If the young (no number stated) obtained from the pair were in fact yellow it can only mean that the Blue cock was actually "split" for White.

We know that Blue/White to Yellow gives the expectation of 50% Green/White and 50% Yellow/White young with the percentage of each varying from one extreme to the other. Should there have been only a few chicks from the pair, which is most probable, they could well have been yellow. It is known that Yellows were paired with Blues at that time and with this particular pair it seems that the Blue could have carried the White character. What I think is rather unusual is that actual White birds did not seem to have appeared during the course of time from such matings. White birds did not put in an appearance until a great many years later.

Breeding

For quite a considerable period of time Blue Budgerigars slipped into obscurity and it was R. Pauvvels of Brabant, Belgium, who brought them to light again, breeding his birds from Dutch stock. It does not seem to be certain exactly when R. Pauvvels began to breed Blues, but it was many years prior to his exhibiting three birds at the Horticultural Hall London Show on 25th-28th November 1910, and D. Seth-Smith exhibited one of Pauvvell's birds at the Zoological Society's meeting on 29th November in the same year. These were the first Blue Budgerigars to be seen in Great Britain and, as would be expected, caused great excitement amongst Budgerigar and Foreign Bird breeders.

Now back to the Blue hen bred from the same pair mentioned in van

Figure 3.1 Greywing Cobalt, Greywing Light Blue and a Blue.
From: *The Budgerigar in Captivity* by Denys Weston

der Snickt's report as having yellow on head and tail. This description tallies with the birds we know today as **Yellow-faced Blues** and if this is correct she must have been the very first Yellow-faced Blue to have been bred. It was over fifty years later that Yellow-faced Blue strains reappeared (!) and were established. This is not the end of the story, as it is said that the Yellow-faced Blue hen and her pure Blue brother were bred from the same light green coloured parents. We now know that green coloured birds cannot be split for *both* Blue and Yellow-faced Blue at the same time and therefore the two birds could not have come from the same parents, unless two separate mutations had occurred. Further information about these birds and their parents does not seem to have been recorded. It must be concluded that the Yellow-faced Blue strain was not established. If the colour of the two young birds was as stated, then one possibility is that the two Green birds that produced the Blue cock were not the same as those which gave the Yellow-faced Blue hen. In those early days of Budgerigar breeding, birds were not ringed, accurate records were not kept and breeding was carried out on the colony system, so information and pedigrees were not always very reliable.

Introduction to Britain

During 1912 R. Pauvvels' collection of Budgerigars was sold and Blues were prices from £12-£15 per pair according to age. A number of these Blue pairs came to Great Britain and were used to found the first Blue strains in this country. Young from a pair of Blues were first reared in Great Britain by C. Pelham Sutton of Putney, London, in 1912. The young Blues left their nest on 31st December just making that year! It is also known they were bred here in 1913 by the Rev. H.D. Astley of Brinsop Court, C. Pelham Sutton of Putney and others from birds of Belgian stock. The first Blue to be bred in Great Britain from green coloured (**Blue-bred Green**) parents was in February 1914 from a pair in A. Pulsford's Devon aviaries. This breeder produced Blues from his Blue-bred Greens for a number of seasons. Another early breeder of Blue-bred Greens and Blues was John W. Marsden of Heysham, Lancs, with whom I had the pleasure of meeting and discussing Budgerigar breeding and their history on a number of occasions.

As previously mentioned in Chapter 2, John Marsden was a great believer in the Blue-bred theory and it is quite understandable why this was so when taking into consideration his first experience with the Blue character that was carried by his green coloured birds. Amongst other prominent breeders of Blue Budgerigars at that time were Mrs. Dalton-Burgess, Mrs. Ransom, W.R.H. Bearly, G.F. Hedges and D. Seth-Smith.

The following extract from Neville W. Cayley's *Budgerigars in Bush and Aviary* 1933 indicates how Blue Budgerigars came to their ancestral home:

> Percy Peir of Sydney, Australia, sends the following interesting notes 'the first intimation received by me of the raising of the Blue Budgerigar was from R. Pauvvels of Brabant, Belgium, with whom I regularly corresponded over a number of years, and about 1906 in one of his letters I recollect him writing to say that he had been breeding Blues for many years.

A.E.W. de B. Wachmann of Beecroft, New South Wales, writes:

> The first Blue Budgerigars, if you could call them such, were brought to Australia by Joseph Ellis for the Zoo about 1918. They were very washy in appearance and turned out failures. In 1920 Fred Mayer brought out five pairs of Blues, Heumann and self bought a pair each, and three pairs were sent to Fred Smith of Brisbane. Most of this consignment developed French Moult and only a few were bred from. Some were forwarded to C. Lienau of Adelaide, who was most successful.

This extract shows that even as late as the early 1920's stocks of Blue Budgerigars in Europe were inbred and rather on the delicate side. This may have been brought about by breeders being afraid to outcross their Blues to Greens or Yellows in case they 'lost' the blue colour.

THE FIRST WHITES

It will have been seen that although Yellow and Blue Budgerigars had been breeding for quite a number of years, it was not until 1920 that the first White was bred in Great Britain. According to Allen Silver in *Budgerigar Bulletin* No. 19 of December 1931:

> Although Russ, page 251 in the Schultze translation of the speaking Parrots refers to a White Budgerigar, the first occurrence here is that of the one bred by the late H.D. Astley (27th September 1920) at Brinsop Court; this young bird came from two blue coloured birds. In the aviaries where Whites appeared once or twice and Yellows in a mixed collection of blue and green coloured birds.

We now know that the expectation of Whites from two Blue/Whites is one in four, from a Blue/White and a Green/White is one in eight and from two Green/Whites one in sixteen. We can conclude from this that during this early period of Budgerigar breeding the chance of two Blue/Whites being mated was small and the possibility of Whites from two Green/Whites was even more slender. When Dr. H. Duncker revealed the Mendelian Principles of Heredity to the Fancy, the production of Whites and all colours became a straightforward breeding exercise. The White is, incidentally, classed as a combination rather than a mutation.

Figure 3.2   Light Blue, Olive Green, Mauve, Cobalt.
From: *The Budgerigar in Captivity* by Denys Weston

47

DARK GREENS

It was in 1915 that the next mutation, the Dark Green, was recognised and established in the aviaries of Blanchard Bros. of Toulouse, France. Research has shown that a preserved skin of a wild-caught Budgerigar that is dark green in colour is in the collection at the Natural History Museum, London.

This raises the possibility that the Dark Green mutation first occurred in the wild and then was recognised in captivity when breeding took place with some wild-caught stock. It is known that Budgerigars trapped in Australia were used to cross into European captive bred strains to help to prevent inbreeding and strengthen the strains.

There are therefore two ways in which Blanchard's Dark Green strain came about: one is that it was a purely captive mutation, and the other that it originated from a wild-caught mutant breeding in captivity. We know that the colour of ordinary Dark Greens can vary considerably, with some being much paler than others. If a wild-caught mutant was one of the paler Dark Greens it could well have passed unnoticed by the trappers when caught in a batch of richly coloured Light Greens. However when the Blanchard Dark Greens came about they were in the course of time to make a far reaching impact on the whole of the Budgerigar colour mutations, as they introduced a new darkening element.

Dark Greens have also been called Laurel Greens and Satin Greens. From his Dark Greens, Blanchard in 1916 produced Olive Greens and as we now know this was the logical sequence when two Dark Green birds are paired together.

COBALTS AND MAUVES

Stemming from this mutation (the dark character) in the Green series came their Blue counterparts: first, the Cobalts in 1920 and then the Mauves quickly following, both appearing in the Blanchard aviaries. A further extract from Allen Silver in *Budgerigar Bulletin* No. 19 throws some light on these early breedings.

> George Hedges when in charge of the collection of Mme. Lecallier bred Cobalts in 1923 and some were sold to the late Mrs. Dalton Burgess; the following year she exhibited one as a Royal Blue Budgerigar in the February Crystal Palace Show A light blue Budgerigar having a cobalt rump described as an Iris was bred by Blanchard in 1922.
>
> In 1924 the late Mrs. Dalton Burgess bred Mauves from Cobalts which in the immature plumage she termed 'French Greys' and at this period certain types of Mauves were also described as lilacs and lavenders. From 1919 until her death I visited her on many occasions and was in frequent consultation with her. It was there I saw the first Dark Olives from France.

DEEPLY SUFFUSED YELLOWS

Up to this point the origins of the Yellow, Lutino, Blue and Dark mutations have been discussed as known from recorded information. The time and place of the appearance of the next mutation, the Greywing or Apple Green, Satinettes and Jade as they were originally called is somewhat hazy. It is highly probable that certain specimens which were called Apple Greens, Satinettes and Jades (Greywing Greens), were what we now know as **deeply suffused Yellows**. These deeply suffused Yellows do have distinct wing markings and a definite body suffusion, and look quite different to the exhibition type Yellows or the lightly suffused kinds. This idea is supported by Allen Silver in *Budgerigar Bulletin* No. 19 where he writes:

> The green greywing as we know it today seems on account of its variable external appearance to have arisen as far as records go in 1920, although I and several of my bird keeping acquaintances seem to have observed it in mixed consignments of yellow coloured birds. This form was regarded as an objectionable exhibition yellow. Mr. G.F. Hedges bred one in 1920 and 1921 apparently from blue coloured and yellow coloured agents. M. Blanchard says his father obtained this bird from two green coloured birds previous to the War, and at the same time some yellows. Blanchard calls them 'jades'. In 1925 in Germany they were referred to as May green Budgerigars and previously here as 'Apple Greens' . . . The first sky

Figure 3.3　**Cobalt Cock** — the first Australian Cup winner (bred and owned by S. E. Terrill, South Australia in the 1930's).

blue greywing I saw was shown by Mr. Hedges as a 'Pearl' in 1928. When on a visit to Herr C.H. Cremer, Bremen, in 1928 I saw at Halle two young ones which he had procured from Vienna; they were produced by pairing two birds of the category green/blue-yellow-white. The parents of these green birds were raised by Mr. Grazl of Vienna by pairing blue coloured birds with yellow coloured birds. A Mrs. H. Weiss of Graz bought birds from Mr. Grazl and obtained sky blue greywings at the same period as Mr. Grazl. Mr. Grazl was both a dealer and a breeder and at the same period that some of his birds came originally from England. Wings of two sky blue greywings were sent to me the same year for examination arising from an English source.

In the *Budgerigar Bulletin* No. 32 of December 1934 Dr. H. Steiner wrote in an article*:

Apple-Green or Greywing Green can be proved to have existed in Germany and Belgium as far back as the years 1875 and 1879.

Allen Silver says that Greywing Greens were of variable external appearance and were also obtained in mixed consignments of yellow coloured birds. This indicates quite clearly that some of these birds seen at that time were in fact deeply suffused Yellows which would naturally appear from these cross matings. A deeply suffused Yellow would stand out quite distinctly in a mixed batch of more or less clear yellow birds. Nevertheless, some time in the early 1920's definite Greywing Green mutations did occur and probably in several countries at about the same time.

It was in the *Budgerigar Bulletin* No. 4 of March 1928 that I was mentioned as having brought up the exhibition position of the Jade and Apple Green at **The Budgerigar Club's** Annual General Meeting on 4th February 1928. The first definite colour descriptions of Apple Greens (Greywing Greens) were given in the Colour Committee's report and, with my letter, in the *Budgerigar Bulletin* No. 5 of June 1928.

The 'Pearl' Budgerigar mentioned by Allen Silver was shown in February 1928 at the Crystal Palace Show by G.F. Hedges, winning the **Any Other Colour Class** and awarded the Special for **Best Budgerigar in Show**. I well remember seeing this fine bird and remarking to my great friend, the late R.J. Watts of Cambridge, how akin it was in markings to the Apple Greens (Greywing Greens) I was exhibiting in the same class. My Apple Green (Greywing Green) strain originated from Apple Greens (Greywing Dark Greens) which appeared in nests during 1925 from the crossing of a Light Green cock to an Olive Green hen.

This quote from an Article I wrote in *The Budgerigar Bulletin* No. 12 of March 1930 gives the history of these Greywings:

*This was based on one that appeared in *Ornithologie und Wissenschaft* of 15th August 1933.

50

A number were bred in my aviaries in 1925 and appeared as a mutation from Olive bred birds. An Olive hen of unknown pedigree was mated to a pure Green* cock, they produced six young — four Dark Greens and two Dark Apple Greens. The next season this Olive hen was mated to a Green/Blue, produced five young — four Dark Greens and again another Dark Apple Green . . . This variation from the normal event seems to have been brought about through the hen who must have been capable of producing mutations no matter what she was mated to.

I feel I must add here that I still have a few Greywings that have this original mutant strain as their remote ancestors.

There were fierce arguments amongst breeders about the recogntion and naming of this mutation. Fanciers not possessing or having seen Greywing Greens called them mongrels, dirty Yellows and washed out Greens.

In 1928 the Colour Committee of **The Budgerigar Club**, after having carefully examined live specimens together with breeding results decided to recognise and name the new mutation **Apple Green**. It was discovered a little later than the 'Pearl' and Silverwing kinds were not separate varieties, but the Blue counterparts of the Apple Greens. In view of this discovery the mutation was then given the group name of Greywing as suggested by Consul General C.H. Cremer in a letter which appeared in *Budgerigar Bulletin* No. 11 of December 1929 and they were recognised as such.

The first separate class for Apple Greens was at the Crystal Palace Exhibition of February 1929 and it was soon after that classes for them were scheduled at some provincial shows. It did not take very long for Greywings, both Blues and Greens, to become popular exhibition birds and they were soon gaining the highest awards at shows in various parts of the country. From this information it can be stated definitely that **Greywing Green** mutations appeared between 1919 and 1925 and that a **Greywing Blue** (Silverwing) form first appeared in Austria in 1927 and then in Great Britain in 1928.

EFFECTS OF THE NEW MUTATIONS ON BREEDERS

The following extracts selected from breeders' letters that appeared in *Cage Birds* between 1925 and 1927 give a good idea of the lack of general information regarding the inheritance and the colours of Budgerigars that existed amongst their breeders:

---

*This cock mated to a pure Light Yellow hen produced only green coloured cocks and hens.

7th February 1925.

Mrs. Dalton-Burgess did not obtain her French Greys from France. I have known Mr. and the late Mrs. Dalton-Burgess a long time, and have had the pleasure of staying with them and I know she bred two colours, pure French Grey and Lilac, in her own aviaries from other colours.

Re Apple Greens, in 1919 Mrs. Ransom wrote to me: 'I am sending you the Light Green cock Budgie'. This was an Apple Green: she called them Jades.

But Mrs. Dalton-Burgess and I thought Apple Green a better name.

J.W. Marsden, F.Z.S.

*   *   *

14th March 1925.

We are not yet at the end of the Budgerigar's capacity for variation. Whites are quite recent productions, and ought to have their chance.

Again, if Olives and Lavenders are not so bright as Greens and Blues the same might be said of Cinnamon Canaries as opposed to Yellows; and yet these are fully recognised.

Then I heard only the other day of a Chocolate variety having appeared on the Continent, which may be leading in the direction of Red.

The Powder Blues have a distinct suggestion of purple in their plumage, and chocolate and purple blue might make crimson for all we know.

Frank Finn, F.Z.S.

*   *   *

25th April 1925.

There are now several varieties of the old Green Budgerigar, namely, the Yellow, Olive, Grey, Blue, Royal Blue, White, Black, and Apple Green, all of which colour varieties are now firmly established and breed true to colour.

Yellow paired to Yellow breed true to colour but Yellow paired to Green or to any other colour always produces only Green. That is why I think Yellows were first produced by extensive inbreeding. Olive paired to Olive breed true to colour, and so do all other colour varieties when paired to their own colour.

When paired with other colours such as Olive to Blue, or Grey to Blue, the young are almost invariably all Green. There are various ways of producing Blue but the easiest and surest way is to pair Blue to Blue.

A. Gutteridge.

*   *   *

19th December 1925.

. . . Now, we all know there are Yellow, Green, Light Blue, and Dark Blue (Cobalts). The writer also mentions that there are other varieties, such as Greys, Dirty Whites, Mauve, Jades and pure White, 'but until pure colour contrast in colour is fixed, but it is not likely they will be recognised here unless the differences are well marked.'

Apple Greens are much darker and a brighter green than the common green. The Jade have more green in the yellow than the common Yellow. These two colours have been bred true to colour for the past five years.

The so-called Greys, which my friend calls Lilacs, have been bred true to colour for the past two years and are a distinct colour from the blues mentioned.

He also mentions 'Mauves', I have never seen this colour, and I doubt if anyone has or ever will.

I think that the Apple Green, Jade, and Lilac will be recognised, and I certainly think they should be.

In the Budgerigar Club rules a Cinnamon standard is given. This colour we have never seen, and I doubt if we ever shall.

From where do we get the foundation for this colour? You cannot get red-brown from green, yellow, or blue, and, I am sure, not from olive.

W. Palmer.

* * *

16th January 1926.

I have among my Yellow birds that I call bad Yellows, and I have cream coloured birds minus practically all signs of marking, and almost without green on the rump I call these bad Yellows.

Allen Silver, F.Z.S.

* * *

10th July 1926.

In my outdoor aviary I have bred and fully reared a pair of White Budgerigars this season.

Their parents were a pair of my own Blue-bred strain, not specially paired or selected in any way. I find the cock was brother to a Blue of last year, and that was bred in turn from my own Blue-breds.

These young Whites are very pure and not a washed out blue, like some I have seen at shows.

I should have said that the nest the Whites were in contained, as well, one very good pure Blue and three Greens.

Mrs. Alice Chatterton.

* * *

21st August, 1926.

As far as I know cobalt, lilac, violet, purple and mauve, all apply to two shades of blue.

Mr. Hedges produced dark blue birds which he called cobalt; the other shade was produced from these and he called them lilacs.

There are always two shades in a light blue class. We should have four classes for blues, sky blue, dark blue, cobalt and lilac.

Apple Greens should be very light green with light blue tails and mauve undulations. Jades, a soft, very light olive green.

John W. Marsden, Z.F.S.

* * *

26th March 1927.

You will always notice when you breed two different colours together, by a peculiar coincidence the young take after the inexpensive parent; thus Green and Yellow produce Green, Olive and Yellow produce Yellow etc. If a White is bred with another colour, by no chance do you breed white coloured young.

The first White ever produced was bred from Blue-bred Greens, bred by the late Mr. H. Astley, and the second one by Mr. Tom Goodwin, also from Blue-bred Greens.

As previously mentioned, we are only at the beginning of the Budgerigar boom, as in the last few years we have produced ten colours in all — Green, Yellow,

53

Olive, Jade, Apple Green, Blue, Cobalt, Mauve and White, all distinctive and fixed colours.

Cyryl M. Whale.

*   *   *

9th April 1927.

I am sorry I cannot agree with Mr. Denys Weston and Dr. Duncker. When I first commenced building a strain of Blue-bred Budgerigars by crossing with selected Greens, I do not think it had been thought about either here or on the Continent.

I agree that first cross of the Blue to Common Green may produce some birds without the power to breed Blues, but I am not sure it is so with Blue cross Yellow (the Yellow, Yellow-bred).

If breeders keep proper pedigrees it is quite easy to know the percentage of Blue blood. Proof in breeding is of little use.

John W. Marsden, F.Z.S.

*   *   *

28th May 1927.

At the Palace meeting of the members of The Budgerigar Club I am informed that, in his lecture Professor Hans Duncker stated that it was not possible to breed Yellows from pure Blues, and I believe this to be generally understood to be so.

In one of my aviaries, containing five pairs·of Blues I bred last season Whites, Greens and Yellows. There is no doubt that the latter colour came from Blues as I am breeding Blues from them this season having 50% in the first nest.

I must state that the Yellows are mated to Blue-bred Greens.

W.J. Child.

*   *   *

11th June 1927.

Those of your readers who remember my pair of White Budgerigars last season, may be interested to know that I have another pair in a first nest of this year.

Last time they were bred from a paid of Blue-bred Greens, but these are from a Yellow hen and a Blue cock. This is distinctly encouraging, as it proves that the White blood is spreading in my stock.

They are now fully reared and flying in my outdoor aviaries, and in the same nest were two Olive looking Greens and a pale Yellow.

Mrs. Alice Chatterton.

*   *   *

11th June 1927.

The following mating notes from my personal experiences may be of interest to others now taking up the hobby.

Blue to Green have produced only Blue-bred Greens. Blue to Blue-bred Greens with one Blue parent have only produced Blue-bred Greens.

Blue to Blue-bred Greens, with one Blue parent, and one Blue grandparent, have produced a fairly level number of Blues and Blue-bred Greens.

Blue to Blue-bred Greens, with one Blue parent, one Blue grandparent, and one Blue great grandparent, have produced a considerably greater number of Blues than Greens. Blue-bred Greens of similar breeding to the above have consistently

produced some Blues when paired together.

These remarks have applied equally to the Blue and Olive crosses in my aviaries.

Norton H. Danby.

*　　*　　*

These extracts from letters written by prominent breeders of the time show how confused they were regarding the inheritance of the then known colour characters in Budgerigars. During this period the Mendelian theory of Budgerigar inheritance was becoming to be more widely known amongst a growing section of Budgerigar breeders. Nevertheless, the old idea of Blue-breds died hard and it was only when the Mendelian principle was so definite that the 'pedigree' breeders accepted the idea.

Colours Available

Now reverting back to **Greywing Greens**; the arrival and spread of this mutation added six new colour varieties to the twelve already existing. This made eighteen separate colour forms, all independent of each other which could not be formed into composite kinds. The Lutino mutation that appeared in the 1870's had not been established at that period otherwise the list of colours would have been increased by Albinos and Lutinos.

With all these new colours bird breeders were attracted to the production of Budgerigars and this trend was helped considerably by the availability of scientific knowledge of the colour inheritance that was appearing in the Fancy literature in various parts of the world. The majority of Budgerigars in this country were now being bred under strictly controlled conditions as opposed to the older method of colony breeding. By breeding under control any mutations of colours that appeared could be quickly spotted and developed on a scientific basis.

THE CINNAMON

When a mutation appeared in 1931 which at first glance seemed to be very similar to the now extensively bred Greywings, its genetical make-up was solved by the well established Mendelian theory. The first British breeder, A.D. Simms of Potters Bar, Middlesex, originally thought the birds he had bred were Greywings. They were all hens and he, thinking them to be Greywings mated them to Greywing cocks and to his utter surprise all the young these pairs produced were normal looking Greens. The following passage from a little book I wrote in 1934 under the title of *Budgerigars and how to breed Cinnamonwings* gives the particulars of the breeding of the Simms' Cinnamonwings as told to me by Mr. Simms during our talks:

In 1931, Mr. A.D. Simms, of Potter's Bar, paired *inter se* some dark green coloured birds which he had bred from an Olive and a Greywing Light Green (this latter could have possibly been a Cinnamonwing). They produced, amongst others, eight Cinnamonwing hens, both light and dark green coloured bodies. During the 1932 breeding season he, together with Mr. Porter of Codicote, who obtained two of these birds from Mr. Simms, paired their hens to various Whites and 'split' Whites and obtained only normally coloured birds. I first came into contact with Cinnamons when Mr. Porter came to me for advice with regard to his Greywing Dark Green coloured hens that were not producing Greywing young. He was good enough to bring with him one of these hens and some of their progeny by Cobalt/White cocks for my inspection. The young were of all shades of the normal colours and not one had the slightest resemblance to a Greywing. At the first glance the hen appeared to be just a good Greywing Dark Green, but on closer examination it could be seen that her undulations were abnormal, having a decided Cinnamon look, and also the quills of the primary and secondary flight feathers were dark reddish brown.

Sex Linkage

It soon became evident from the breeding results obtained from this particular strain of birds by F. Porter, R.J. Watts, A.A. Collier and myself who had obtained birds from the original Simms' stock that they were not Greywings, but a new form with a sex-linked inheritance. Close examination of their flight and other feathers revealed that the usual black colour pigment was absent, leaving only the brown (cinnamon) colour visible, so they were named at the time Cinnamonwings. These first birds were all of the **Green** series, but it was not long before **Cinnamonwing Blues, Cinnamonwing Cobalts** and **Cinnamonwing Mauves** began to put in an appearance.

Their soft colours quickly endeared them to a large number of breeders and exhibitors and they were crossed with other colours that existed at that time. The results of these cross pairings soon revealed the fact that it was possible to have a Cinnamonwing form of all the other kinds. It was then realised by experimental colour breeders that the prefix Cinnamonwing was somewhat cumbersome and in certain cases incorrect. After weighing up the *pros* and *cons* the Colour Committee of **The Budgerigar Club** unanimously agreed that the prefix Cinnamon would be more appropriate. This was approved and soon adopted by breeders in all parts of the world.

The appearance of the sex-linked Cinnamon character had a very profound effect on Budgerigar breeding as a whole. It was the first sex-linked colour to become generally available to breeders and the young Cinnamons could be identified immediately they were hatched. Up to the appearance of the Cinnamon character, with the exception of the Albino (Lutino) character, it had not been possible to identify the sex of certain baby birds on hatching. When Cinnamons of any colour are first hatched, their eyes behind the covering of skin appear purplish-pink, whereas with ordinary birds it is definitely blackish. As the young Cinnamons develop their eye colour deepens, but never assumes the blackness of ordinary birds, and when viewed at an angle in a good bright light a reddish gleam can be observed. This is a characteristic of the cinnamon (fawn) coloured birds of any species.

This method of early identification was most useful to breeders endeavouring to increase their stock of this new attractive sex-linked mutation. Being sex-linked, it is possible to tell which young from Normal/Cinnamon cocks and Normal hens were Cinnamons and the breeder could adjust the young accordingly. The Cinnamon character had a further usefulness to breeders of pet birds where young cock birds are in great demand. Cinnamon cocks of any colour paired to Normal hens produce all Cinnamon hens and *all normally* coloured cocks. The fact that it is possible to sex the birds early is a great help to pet bird breeders in selecting young cocks to be trained as talking household pets, before they leave the nest.

The production of known cock birds from sex-linked colour matings is also applicable to the other sex-linked mutations of Budgerigars. Young cocks from Albino, Lutino and Lacewing cocks mated to Normal hens give cocks that can be recognised on hatching by their normal eye colour, and those from Opaline and Slate cocks to Normal hens when they are feathering.

Appearance in Other Countries

In addition to the British Cinnamon mutation in 1931 there were others reported from Europe, Australia, America and South Africa during the following few years. In due course of time it was proved beyond all doubt that these different mutations all behaved in the same manner of reproduction and could be crossed together, as with the different Greywing mutations. It often seems that when a mutation occurs in one area it will occur again in several places within a short space of time.

Information in most reports on the actual dates of the appearance of Cinnamons in other countries were somewhat sketchy, although there was no doubt of the mutation occurring, and in due course becoming established strains. A letter I received from Tom Treloar of Melbourn, Australia, dated 21st January 1937, contained a great deal of interesting information on Australian Budgerigar breeding. Amongst the items is an account of the first Australian Cinnamonwings (Cinnamons):

Now perhaps a little history would be of interest to you. There has been much written about the creation of the Cinnamonwings in Australia, but there is one side of it that is not generally known. There was a woman in Adelaide some three and a half to four years ago (about 1936-37) who was not a member of any Budgerigar or Bird Society. This particular woman decided she would like to have a couple of pairs of Budgies under the back veranda, so went to one of the bird shops and bought a pair of ordinary Greens at *random* for 3 shillings (15p). These birds were duly mated and placed in a small cage — the pair had two nests — all green tinted birds with cinnamon wings. The woman did not like these birds on account of their washed out body colour, and she was so disgusted that she sold all the young ones to Mr. Mackay a bird dealer of Gawler Place, Adelaide, for 1 shilling and 6 pence (7½p) or 2 shillings (10p) per pair. Not knowing any difference Mackay sold them at 6 shillings (30p) and seven shillings (35p) a pair. Well, Mr. S.E. Terrell (a well known Australian breeder) got to hear of these particular birds and he did what I would have done in the circumstances — he jumped into his car and went straight to Mackay's shop and succeeded in buying the last Cinnamonwing for 4 shillings (20p), and made enquiries and found out who had purchased the others. He promptly went round and bought up the lot and I understand the last bird cost him either £7 or £9, but nevertheless he got the lot and started off to mate them together and has continued to produce poor body coloured birds ever since. Therein my friend is the origin of the Australian Cinnamonwings.

It is quite clear from the above extract that breeders had expected Cinnamons to have the same depth of body colour as Normal Greens, hence the mention of poor body colour in the letter. The account does not give the actual number or sex of the Cinnamon young produced, beyond the fact that the adults raised two nests. There must have been birds of both sexes, as it also states that Mr. Terrell mated them together. This rules out the possibility of all the young being hens as this would be possible if the original Light Green cock had been a Cinnamon carrier. This is what happened with the Simms' Cinnamon mutation, where all the Cinnamons were hens. However, the Australian mutation appeared to give Cinnamons in both sexes, a most unusual occurrence in a sex-linked kind.

Exhibiting the New Mutation

At the Crystal Palace Exhibition, London, in February 1932, G. & J. Hughes, partners of that famous firm of ring manufacturers, exhibited in the **White of Light Suffusion class** a very pale Sky Blue with faint light brown undulations and throat spots. This bird, a hen, was placed second in her class of thirty four entries. She appeared to have been bred during the same period as the Simms' Cinnamons and must have been the very first Cinnamon Budgerigar to be exhibited.

I remember seeing her quite well and she was certainly a nice shapely bird being produced from top quality Normals, but did not at the time connect her with the Green series Cinnamons which I saw and bred some time later. She was what we would call nowadays the Cinnamon form of a White of deep suffusion, but unfortunately she died without issue. This bird is described in an article headed **The Brown Factor** in *Budgerigar Bulletin* No. 21 of June 1932.

It is interesting to note that at this particular Crystal Palace Exhibition in the Light Green cock class there were forty five entries, the Sky Blue cocks numbered forty and the Mauves thirty six. Although Light Green and Sky Blue classses have often exceeded these entry figures, those of the Mauves seldom get beyond single figures even at the largest shows. The first **Cinnamon Mauves** were, incidentally, bred by A.A. Collier then of Luton, Bedfordshire in 1933. In the same year G.F. Porter of Codicote, Hertfordshire paired one of the first Cinnamon hens to a split cock and they bred the first Cinnamon cock bird.

Sex-linked Characteristics

Budgerigar Bulletin No. 25 of January 1933 contains a great deal of information about the new Cinnamonwings (Cinnamons) from various breeders, which makes most interesting reading. From these notes it was obvious that the hereditary nature of the Cinnamon character was not yet fully understood. For instance it was thought that Normal hens could be split for Cinnamon and that Whites and Yellows were not affected by the Cinnamon character. However, in the following Bulletin I was able to publish my own experimental breeding results showing that the Cinnamon character was a sex-linked one and there could be a Cinnamon form of all other varieties.

This finding was supported by several fanciers who had also been breeding with Cinnamon and split birds. Needless to say, the discussions about Cinnamons, and when they first appeared, carried on for some time amongst fanciers and in avicultural literature. During this time Cinnamon birds enjoyed increased support all round, many good strains were developed and the Cinnamon forms of all the other known colours were bred. Amongst those who first exhibited these new Cinnamon birds were R.J. Watts, G.F. Porter, Mr. & Mrs. A.A. Collier, Mrs. D. Wall, Walter Higham, F.R. Waite, Miss V. Scott, Col. Minchin and myself.

Cinnamon specimens of many kinds of birds occur in the wild, and if captured can be formed into domesticated strains of Cinnamons. It might have been so with Budgerigars, as this extract headed *An Old Cinnamonwing* by C.H. Rogers from *Budgerigar Bulletin* No. 36 of December 1935 indicates:

In my note in *Bird Fancy*, **November 9th, 1935, issue, I gave a few details of the discovery of a skin of a Cinnamonwing (Cinnamon) Light Green which had been stuffed for at least fifty years. It was W.P.C. Unwin of Histon, Cambridge, who gave me the information and an introduction to a Mrs. Ellis of Cottenham,**

Figure 3.3 Cyril H. Rogers the original author and famous bird breeder.
Viewing Young birds in his flights

CHAPTER 4

HISTORY OF THE MUTATIONS
II — THE RAINBOW YEARS

The 1930's might well be called the Rainbow years of the Budgerigar, as a whole batch of different colour mutations appeared during that period. These varied coloured mutations certainly had a tremendous influence on the development and spreading of the keeping, breeding and exhibiting of Budgerigars in many parts of the world. If they had not occurred, Budgerigars would most likely not have the great following they have today.

FALLOWS

It was in *Budgerigar Bulletin* No. 19 of December 1931 that a letter appeared giving the first intimation that a new kind of **red-eyed variety** had been bred in America. A Mrs. A.R. Hood of California wrote:

> **I have two pairs of greens, bred from greens. At this time of writing I have, from one pair of greens, four young birds of a yellowish-green, with almost cinnamon-grey wings and tail, and real deep *red* eyes. From two pairs of greens, I have two young; one of which is the same yellowish green, cinnamon-grey wings and tail, and red eyes; the other is a clear canary yellow with no markings anywhere, except what might be called invisible, they are so faint which also has the deep red eyes — a very beautiful bird.**
>
> **Now, I would like to hear if anyone else has raised birds of this description, and what results if any, have been had from breeding them; whether they bred red eye to red eye or otherwise.**

The production of red-eyed birds from three different pairs of Light Greens indicates that this mutation is a recessive one and had occurred some time previously on a half of a chromosome pair and had been passed on to other green birds in the stock. When two birds, both carrying a new recessive colour, are paired together the actual new coloured birds appear. This shows that the American mutation must

61

have actually occurred some time during 1929. The fact that almost clear red-eyed Yellow birds were amongst the young showed that the Green strain also carried the Yellow character. This opened great possibilities, as at that time many green coloured birds were split for Yellow. As the eye colour was described as being deep red it would seem that they were a similar mutation to the **German Fallow**. As far as records go, the **American Fallows** were not established at the time as nothing more was heard of Mrs. Hood's strain of birds, although she had sold them to other breeders.

In an article in *Budgerigar Bulletin* No. 35 of June 1935 Dr. H. Steiner of Zürich writes:

> ... the birds bred by Herr Schumann of Magdeburg in 1932 do not appear to have been the first occurrence of this mutation. Before this, in the year 1929, a Swiss fancier Herr Augustin, of Biel bred a brown winged red-eyed Budgerigar according to the description given must have been a Fallow. It came from the mating of an Olive and a Greywing Green and was a cock ... Unfortunately this bird died in the summer of 1930 without leaving any issue ...

In the Spring of 1933 Herr von Oerzen had a **Fallow Mauve** suddenly appear in a nest from a pair of Cobalts, the other chicks in the clutch were normally coloured. This appears to be a further independent Fallow mutation to that of the Schumann strain.

According to a note that appeared in the *Avicultural Magazine* of October 1933, Herr C. Balser of Darmstadt, Germany, had bred "Yellow" Budgerigars with ruby red eyes, the bars on the wings being brown. He had also bred "White" birds with red eyes and similar brown markings on their wings. This note was quoted in the *Budgerigar Bulletin* No. 27 of October 1933. In the following *Bulletin* No. 28 of December 1933, a further red-eyed mutation was reported by Francis H. Rudkin, who stated that birds similar to those of Herr C. Balser of Germany and Mrs. A.R. Hood of America, with ruby red eyes, had been bred by Mrs. Flowers and Mr. Hood, members of the **Avicultural Society of Australia**. Mr. Rudkin saw the birds himself and said that the most peculiar thing about them was that the ceres were practically alike in both sexes. This Australian mutation was developed and is still being bred successfully in that country.

There was much discussion about these new red eyed birds amongst British Budgerigar breeders, and speculation as to their possibilities was rife. In February of 1934, the production of these red eyed brown marked birds was clarified somewhat by an article in *Der Wellensttich* by Kurt Kokemuller, which was translated for *Budgerigar Bulletin* No. 29 of March 1934 by F.S. Elliott as follows:

The fallow* birds are quite a new variety. In December 1932 Herr Schrapel and I, as joint owners, received these very beautiful birds from the breeder, Herr Schumann of Magdeburg. The birds are golden yellow with undulation markings and throat spots of a definite brown shade. The rump is yellow olive, the feet are pale pink as with the albino and the eyes are red, but not quite such a light red as in the case of the albino. The beak is yellow, the cere of the cocks is not so decidedly blue as in normal cocks but pale bluish purple. They are very fine birds, not in any way weak or small, but of good type and healthy. From breeding tests with these birds it has been ascertained they are split blues . . . Herr Schumann informed me that he obtained the red-eyed birds from mating cobalt to olive and that he obtained such birds in each of three broods. As mutations are so extremely rare they could not have been produced in successive nests, and that both parents, which were possibly brother and sister carried the hidden factor of this new variety.

From this it can be seen that Fallow and Cinnamon are very distinct mutations each owing its coloration to entirely different colour characters.

Introduction to Great Britain

The Fallows quickly multiplied in the hands of their competent German breeders and during June of 1934 the first examples were imported into Great Britain by H.R. Scott, B.S. Campkin, F.G. Simpson and W.P.C. Unwin. I saw these birds soon after they arrived in this country and like all Budgerigar breeders, who saw the mutation for the first time, was amazed at the deep yellow and orange yellow body colour of the **Green birds**.

The **Blue series** of the Fallows, although quite striking are not so attractive to the eye as their Green counterparts. Messrs. Scott and Campkin were the first British breeders to rear Fallows fully, although Messrs. Simpson and Unwin actually hatched out the first young Fallows; these, unfortunately, died in infancy. Several other breeders, including myself, had Fallows from Herr Balser and within a short space of time this variety was producing freely in all colours in various aviaries all over the country.

Exhibiting

When Fallows started appearing on the show benches they created quite a sensation and examples, particularly of the Olive kind, were soon gaining the highest awards at many of the larger shows up and down the country. For some years the Cambridge area was the stronghold of breeders of the Fallow forms and The Budgerigar Society's Patronage Shows in that city always had a wonderful display of the Fallow

*In giving the name fallow, which applies to a class comprising several colours in the same way as the word greywing, I have translated the German word. As Herr Kokemuller puts it: 'as fallow land is uncultivated so the fallow bird is nearly unpigmented or diluted'.

varieties. Some of the teams of Fallows benched during this period were really delightful to look at with their golden orange yellow body colour and clear cut greyish brown markings. The Teams at this time consisted of six birds, three true pairs, six cocks or six hens, all to be matched for size, shape and evenness of colour.

Although the **German Fallows** were the first in the exhibition field of red-eyed varieties, nowadays, however, they are seldom seen at shows. It is difficult to think that in the onset Fallows were winning and being shown quite extensively up and down the country. At the present time some breeders do still have small studs of Fallows and odd specimens find their way to the shows. For instance, at the 1977 Silver Jubilee National Exhibition of Cage and Aviary Birds at Alexandra Palace, I showed for the first time a German Fallow Recessive Pied Violet Green cock and a German Fallow Recessive Pied Cobalt hen. The few other Fallows that were shown during that year were all of the German strain.

Whilst discussing Budgerigar mutations at the 1979 National Exhibition (London) with two very experienced breeders and exhibitors from Australia, Dr.Harold Cooper of Sydney and Roy Scott of New Lambton, New South Wales, I learned that Fallows are still being bred and exhibited quite extensively in that country. It would appear that their Fallows have been developed from the old Australian mutation which is similar in colouring and character to the German kind. No trace can be found of the introduction of German Fallows into Australia so it can be taken that their birds are due to a separate mutation. These Fallows are of excellent quality and fine type and their classes at the shows are also well contested.

ALBINOS AND LUTINOS

Before the Fallows could reach their peak in popularity they had to meet a challenge from further red-eyed kinds: the **clear white Albinos** and the **clear yellow Lutinos**, which had also occurred in Europe whilst the Fallows were being developed.

Developing the Albino

Clear yellow red-eyed birds (Lutinos) have been bred as far back as 1879, although no breeding strains were developed from these examples. However, in Volume I of *Vogel ferner Lander*, a letter from Herr. E. Bohm of Bawerk, Vienna, gave the news that he had hatched an *Albino* Budgerigar, in September 1931, from a pair of Cobalt/Whites. The bird, a hen, was the last of a nest of nine chicks and pure white throughout without any trace of markings, throat spots, or cheek patches.

In *Der Wellensittch* of November 1933, Herr Kurt Kokemuller reported a further Albino being bred from Sky Blues by Herr Fischer of Honow in September 1933. Herr Kokemuller, together with Herr Schrapel, bought the bird and paired her with a White Cobalt cock. This mating produced three Sky Blue hens, three Cobalt hens and one Cobalt cock. The colouring of the young birds rather surprised the breeders as both the parents lacked colour yet all their young were fully coloured Normals.

As we are aware today, this mutant Albino hen was simply masking Normal Sky Blue and when paired to a White Cobalt would naturally give only normally coloured young split for White, with the young cock being the only chick split for Albino.

Sex-Linkage

Judging by the correspondence and articles in the Fancy literature at that time it was not known for certain whether these new Albinos were of a sex-linked inheritance or a Recessive one. The Albinos mentioned above had all been hen birds and that pointed to sex-linkage, which later was to be proved by breeding results. The doubts about the method of inheritance of the Clear red-eyed birds were not so strange as they might first have been thought, as the following notes show.

In 1934 W.E. Higham of Clayton-le-Dale, Lancs, imported a **Yellow Albino** (Lutino) from Europe and paired him in due time with a **Cinnamon White Blue** hen. The first result from this cross was three Dark Yellows and one White Cobalt indicating that their father was a Lutino Yellow Olive. This was not unusual in itself as many of the European rare coloured birds were of the Olive, Dark Green, Mauve or Cobalt kinds. Mr. Higham's bird was certainly of a glorious depth of rich yellow colour, similar to several other Lutinos I had seen in the Cambridge area also of European origin. Herr C. Belser was at that time the main exporter of rare coloured birds from Europe being in close contact with all the breeders of these birds.

Various examples of these imported Clear red-eyed birds were mated together and also to existing normal colours and some of the results obtained were exceedingly puzzling to their breeders. For example, W.E. Higham's **Clear Yellow red-eyed** cock crossed with **Normal** hens gave only normally coloured cocks and hens. These results were contrary to several other similar crosses where Normal cocks and Clear red-eyed hens were produced in line with the usual sex-linked expectations. In some of the other crosses, **Clear red-eyed** cocks to **Clear red-eyed** or **Normal** hens disappointingly produced only normally coloured chicks. It was these latter breeding results that gave

65

the clue to these unusual breeding results: there existed two kinds of Clear red-eyed birds, one sex-linked and the other Recessive.

This discovery came as a relief to breeders who had found the production of Clear red-eyed birds working somewhat contrary to their expectations. Naturally it took several breeding seasons to sort out the pedigrees of the birds resulting from crossing the two distinct Lutino kinds. In the end success was achieved and the two separate varieties were again in production without complications.

To clarify matters, it must be stated here that no visual colour difference could be detected between the non-sex-linked and the sex-linked kinds. For a time it was the non-linked birds that were generally of the best quality and consequently were winning at the shows. As the **sex-linked Lutinos** were easier to breed they forged ahead and, in time, superseded the once all-conquering non-linked Clear red-eyes. Towards the end of the 1940's the non-linked Clear red-eyed strains finally started to disappear and in the end ceased to exist. It is always possible that the non-linked Clear red-eyed mutation may appear once again some time in the future amongst Budgerigar breeding stocks anywhere in the world.

Sex-linked Lutinos now have a tremendous following of enthusiastic breeders and exhibitors and well supported classes of fine richly coloured substantially made birds grace the show benches. **The sex-linked Albinos** have never been as popular as their Yellow counterparts, nevertheless from time to time some exceedingly good shapely Albinos both cocks and hens are shown.

Breeding in Britain

Most of the early Clear red-eyed mutations had occurred and been established in Europe but there were also mutations in this country. The first actual recording of Lutinos in Great Britain was, of course, the famous two bred by C.P.Arthur, as described in Chaper I; unfortunately they were not established.

In an article that appeared in *Cage Birds* W. Watmough reported that T. Mullies of Horsham, Sussex, had bred an Albino hen from a Sky Blue cock and his Light Green/Blue mate and it was hatched in August 1932. The following year she was paired to a Sky Blue cock and produced four Sky Blue hens and one Sky Blue cock. The young cock was paired to one of his sisters and they bred two Sky Blues the sex of which was not stated. The adult Albino hen was not used for further breeding as she had become egg bound and although she recovered she did not seem fit enough for further breeding. No Albinos, apparently, resulted from this particular mutation as there is no mention in any records.

In the Autumn of 1936, I obtained a **Lutino** hen that had been bred in the June of that year from a pair of unrelated ordinary exhibition Light Yellows owned by a Mr. Doggett of Sawbridgeworth, Herts. The adult Light Yellow pair had nine chicks in all from two nests consisting of the Lutino and eight normal Light Yellows. Mr. Doggett had bred from this strain of Light Yellows for a number of years without introducing fresh stock, therefore this Lutino can be taken as a distinct mutation. I had her for several breeding seasons and she gave me a large number of young with various cock birds.

One of her many mates was a sex-linked Lutino of German origin and all their young, both cocks and hens, were Lutinos. This particular mating proved that the Doggett mutation was of the same kind as the one from Europe, which is now widely bred. Mutations similar to those already existing can occur at any time and can easily be overlooked as being something new.

PIEDS

During the first half of the 1930's other mutations put in an appearance and in due course most were developed into breeding strains both in Great Britain and overseas. In the March *Budgerigar Bulletin* No. 20 of 1932 two new kinds are mentioned.

The first of them were two **green and yellow birds** which were displayed at the 1929 Crystal Palace, London, and belonged to Madame Le Callier of France. I remember seeing these birds and they were what we today call Pieds, but could have been either Dominant or Recessive as their colouring could have fitted either kind. Their eye colour was not observed at that period, as it was not known there was any eye colour different to red or black.

In the same note mention is made of a **green and blue Bi-colour**, belonging to Herr C. Balser with its colours equally divided down the centre. On another page four more bi-coloured birds are reported and also that one cock had been paired to a Normal hen and had produced nine normally coloured youngsters. This, and subsequent results, made it clear that the bi-coloured phenomenon was not an inheritable one but something that appeared by change through a chromosome mishap.

In the *Budgerigar Bulletin* No. 23 of December 1932 I gave a list of seventeen **Bi-colours (Half-siders)** that had been recorded in Budgerigar literature in several countries up to that time. Speculation amongst breeders as to whether it was possible to reproduce these strange colourings was world-wide and much was written about their possibilities. It was not until 1935 that the cause was revealed in a paper,

'Autosomal Colour Mosaics in the Budgerigar' by Professor F.A.E. Crew and Rowena Lamy appearing in the *Journal of Genetics*, Vol. XXX No. 2 March 1935. This enlightening paper explained the genetical reason for the appearance of Half-Siders and also birds of unequal colour divisions (**Mosaics**), and why they do not reproduce their particular pattern. Half-Siders always make interesting exhibits and some of the specimens with perfect lines of demarcation are most attractive.

An interesting account of the breeding result from a pair of Half-siders was given in the German magazine *AZ - Nachrichten* No.1 of 1966. The pair consisted of a cock **Recessive Pied**, half dark green and half yellow-faced cobalt and a hen Recessive Pied half light green and half yellow-faced sky blue. In the space of two years this pair raised thirty-seven young Recessive Pieds, consisting of seven dark green, sixteen sky blue, one light green and three cobalts. Although both birds clearly showed the yellow-faced character in half of their plumage no visual yellow-faced young were bred nor were any Half-siders. This mating result supports the fact that the Half-Sider colour phase cannot be inherited.

At the 1930 Crystal Palace show F. Turnber of Stratford, London, exhibited a **Blue and White Pied** hen in the A.O.C. class. This hen was bred from a pair of normally coloured Sky Blues and eventually passed into the hands of Lieut. Col. A.H. Wall of Marlborough for experimental breeding purposes. Once again the mutation was not established, although I think some young were bred from the bird.

The next mention of Pied Budgerigars was in the September *Budgerigar Bulletin* No. 22 of 1932 when Denys Weston of Dawlish, Devon, reported having obtained a **Cobalt and White Pied** hen from a breeder in Scotland. A half tone block of this bird appeared in that Bulletin. No further Pieds were apparently obtained from either of these Cobalt and White or Blue and White Pied hens.

W.G. Bowden of Christchurch, Hants, obtained in 1931 a **Green and Yellow Pied** cock which he paired to a White Blue hen and obtained eleven young. Two of the young were Green and Yellow Pieds and one a Sky Blue with a white tick at the back of its head. This result showed that this particular Pied character was a Dominant one but for one reason or another it was not perpetuated.

Danish Recessive Pied

It was not until 1932 that a definite Pied mutation occurred and was established in Denmark. This soon became known as the Danish Recessive Pied, although at one time they were called **Finnish Pieds**

68

because the first birds into this country actually came from Finland.

The first mutant occurred in a mixed coloured collection breeding as a colony, and therefore it was not possible to ascertain the exact parentage. One of the first ornithologists to realise that these green and yellow coloured birds were the result of an important new mutation was Herr C. af Eneljelm, then Curator of Helsinki Zoological Gardens, Finland. It was through his interest and experiments that the blue and white Recessive Pieds were evolved and the mutation firmly fixed in Europe. Writing in the *Budgerigar Bulletin* of December 1963 Herr C. af Enehjelm said:

> . . . the first known Danish Pied appeared at a bird show in Copenhagen in 1932, exhibited in a flight with some normal Light Greens. The bird in question was a young Pied Light Green cock, a small slim bird, pied green and yellow, the green colour predominating.
>
> The bird was bought by two of my friends K. Riis-Hansen and the late A. Reddersen, in partnership, and on my advice mated to a White Blue hen, which seemed to be the most suitable bird for a test mating. All the young from this mating were light green appearance, genetically Light Green/White Pied.
>
> The following season some of these young were mated together and one hen back to her father. From these matings several Pieds in green and sky blue were bred. Some of these Pied Greens and Pied Blues were very pale green or blue. They were Pied Yellows and Pied White Blues respectively, which we did not, however, realise at that time . . .
>
> During the war I lost sight of the Pieds and their number diminished considerably. Both of the original breeders gave up the colour, and I believe that it as in the first place to the credit of that well known Danish breeder, Walter Langberg, of Copenhagen, that the colour was saved . . .

In January of 1939 I obtained the following information from one of the original breeders of Danish Recessive Pieds, Herr Kai Riis-Hansen of Copenhagen, Denmark:

> When a friend and I were visiting a Cage Bird Show in 1932 we saw a pied light yellow and green cock Budgerigar. My friend took it to his aviaries and I gave him a white sky blue hen and we had only one brood that season and were most surprised that all the youngsters were ordinary looking light greens.
>
> For a period of two years, I saw nothing of the results, so I claimed my part of the collection that consisted of three pied birds, two of which were yellow and green and one almost snow white with slight bluish suffusion on the lower part of the body. (This was undoubtedly the first white form of the recessive pied to be produced) . . .
>
> The following year I paired the pied fathers with their daughters and got pieds and green/pieds, both cocks and hens. I also tried to match green/pied with green/pied and had in the first round three chicks all pied. At present I have six pied birds all like the original pied green and yellow. I am looking forward to this breeding season and will let you know the result.

The second World War period, with its associated complications, delayed the introduction of these Pieds into Great Britain until 1948. Herr Eneljelm kindly sent me from Finland, two **green and yellow Pieds** and a **Normal** split for Pied and from these three birds I was able

Figure 4.1　View of an Australian's Aviary near Sydney, in the 1930's

70

to found the first Recessive Pied strain in this country. These birds were prolific and it was not long before small pockets of Danish Recessive Pieds were breeding successfully in many aviaries. I exhibited the first examples I bred at the Cambridge Show in 1950 and these were, in fact, the first known Danish Recessive Pieds to be shown in this country.

Because of the highly distinct type that was associated with the Recessive Pied colouring it made it extremely difficult to bring them up to the *standard* of the then existing exhibition type. Because of this fact most of the breeding of Danish Recessive Pieds passed into the hands of colour and aviary breeders who used the Danish Recessive Pieds to add colour and variety to their collections. This meant that Danish Recessive Pieds were often paired together or to split birds with some years of Danish Recessive Pied ancestry resulting in the standardising of the long slender type of bird. It was quite some long time before a few keen Danish Recessive Pied breeders realised that the only way in which to improve the breed was to pair the best of them to pure first class Normals. The first cross young resulting from such pairings were then paired back to selected Danish Recessive Pieds that gave a percentage of Danish Recessive Pieds showing a slight improvement in type. This method has persisted to the present day and has resulted in a very drastic improvement in overall quality of Danish Recessive Pieds now seen.

The actual **colour pattern** of Danish Recessive Pieds can vary very considerably ranging from birds showing only about 5% to 10% of dark colour to those showing 10% to 15% light colour. When Danish Recessive Pieds were first imported, the green and blue shades on their body area were extremely rich and deep with an iridescent sheen. This brilliance of colour was made even more noticeable by the dull black of the markings shown on wings, back, neck and head area. After some years of cross pairing with other colour varieties particularly Greys and Grey Greens the colour brilliance has been reduced considerably in many examples.

In September of 1947 I had a report from E.B. Hudelson, Secretary of **The American Budgerigar Society,** telling me of a **Pied Blue hen** that had been bred the previous year by a Mrs. E.B. Norwood of Austin, Texas, America. From a written description and black and white photographs (see page 72) of this hen it appeared she was coloured similarly to the Danish Recessive Pied mutation. The colour of her eyes was, however, not given so it was impossible to prove whether or not she was a like mutation to the Danish Recessive Pied.

She was a good breeder and paired to a White Blue cock gave quite a number of young both Blue and White Blue showing that she was herself split for White. Unfortunately, no further details of this bird or her progeny seem available and it is not known if any further Pied birds were

71

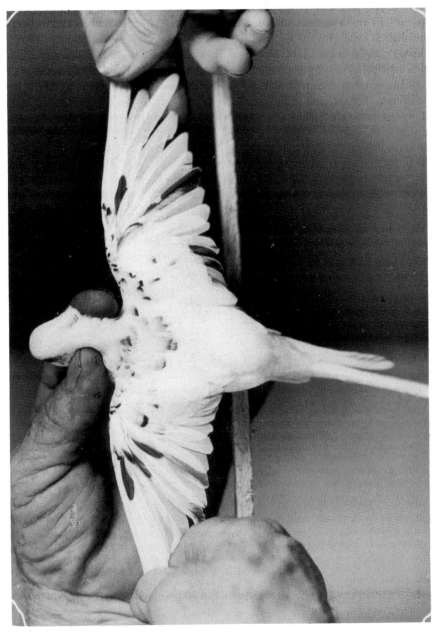

Figure 4.2 An American Pied Budgerigar.

ever bred from this strain. This Pied hen was bred before any live specimens of the Danish Recessive Pieds had reached either Great Britain or America. There was a greater delay in the introduction of this breed to Australia. Because of a ban on the import and export of birds which has lasted for many years, Australian Budgerigar breeders have had to rely, with few exceptions, on native mutations for all their colour changes. This has meant that a small number of mutations known in other parts of the world are not available in Australia.

Recently I heard of rather an interesting account of how the Danish Recessive Pied did, eventually, reach Australia. It would appear that a member of the crew of a vessel berthed in an Australian harbour had on board a pair of Budgerigars breeding in a cage. A visitor to the ship saw the birds and, being a fancier, realised they were Pieds of a different kind to those with which he was familiar. To his delight he discovered that the pair were busy incubating a clutch of fertile eggs. In due course the clutch was transferred to a nest on the land where they were hatched and reared to full maturity. I was not told the number, sex or colours, of these young Recessive Pieds but they undoubtedly formed the nucleus of the strains of Recessive Pieds found in Australia today.

Clearflighted Pied

The Danish Recessive Pied mutation occurred during 1932, but did not reach Great Britain until 1948. During that period, and whilst the second world war was raging in Europe, another Pied mutation, the Clearflighted was developed in the aviaries of Mon. R. Raemaker of Brussels, Belgium.

Examples of these Continental Clearflighted were imported into Great Britain some years prior to the Danish Recessive Pieds and were being bred quite successfully in various colour forms. Although I had seen odd examples of Continental Clearflights that had found their way into this country it was from Mon. Raemaker himself that I received accurate details of this interesting patterned mutation.

Before the end of World War II I received a letter, together with two photographed drawings of the Clearflights that were brought over from Belgium by a British soldier coming home on leave. As it will be seen on page 75, these photographs depict perfectly coloured specimens of a **Whiteflighted Opaline**, called a White Flight-feathers clear-backed Opalin and a **Whiteflighted Normal**, called here a White-flight feathers (Budgerigar). These photographs show that well marked birds have all clear flight and tail feathers and a clear patch at the top of the neck, otherwise they are coloured like their normal counterparts.

Mon. Raemaker said it had taken him several years of selective

73

breeding from the original birds, which had only a few clear yellow feathers in various places, to produce the perfectly marked specimens in Green, Blue and Opaline. He said they were Dominant in their inheritance but their breeding results were variable, and this fact was soon discovered by breeders in Great Britain. During the early part of their development here some very fine well marked birds were seen in the aviaries of breeders and at various shows up and down the country.

Clearflights were quite popular up to the time when Danish Recessive Pieds came into fashion with **Dominant Australian Pieds** appearing on the scene at the same time, causing interest in Clearflights to wane. Nevertheless, for some years there were breeders of Clearflights and with their efforts they improved very considerably the substance and type of their birds. Even today there are small numbers of Clearflights in breeders' aviaries, but it is seldom a specimen is seen on the show benches.

Dark-eyed Clears

Some time in the last 1940's and early 1950's, information came from Europe that Albinos and Lutinos with black eyes were being bred. For a time no details were available to the Budgerigar Fancy in Great Britain until some specimens were imported and birds offered for sale in *Cage Birds*. At first it was thought that such birds could only be bred from the mating together of two black-eyed Albinos or Lutinos, but this was later proved to be incorrect. After a time experimental pairings gave the answer to the question, as it was discovered that the so-called **Black-eyed Albinos and Lutinos** were really a combination of the Danish Recessive Pied and the Dominant Continental Clearflighted. It was seen that these birds did not have black eyes but the deep plum coloured eyes of the Danish Recessive Pied and they became known as **Dark-eyed Clears**.

In fact these birds are the Danish Recessive form of the Continental Clear-flighted and as yet no one has been able to give an explanation why two different Pied forms when paired together can produce a percentage of pure Yellow and pure White birds. It is now known that by mating Danish Recessive Pieds to Clear-flighted, and then mating the Clear-flighted young of this pairing back to Danish Recessive Pieds a proportion of their young are Dark-eyed Clears.

The original Dark-eyed Clears were quite small birds and consequently did not make a favourable impression with exhibiting Fanciers. A few examples are shown each year at various shows, including The Budgerigar Society Club Show and the National Exhibition. One breeder who has produced a considerable number of

74

A. **Whiteflighted Opaline**   B. **Whiteflighted Normal**

Figure 4.3 Belgian Clearflights of the 1940's.

75

Dark-eyed Clears for the past decade is W.A.T. Morecombe of Warminster and has regularly exhibited these birds at the National Exhibition. He tells me he has found it is very hard to increase the size of the Dark-eyed Clears because of the difficulty in obtaining good, large breeding stock. However, now that the Recessive Pieds have been improved to such an extent, it should not be very long before this improvement can be reflected in the Dark-eyed Clears.

Australian Dominant Banded Pied

Whilst the Danish Recessive Pied and Continental Clearflighted mutations were being developed in Europe a further striking mutation had appeared in Australia — the Dominant Banded Pied. At one time it was thought that these Australian Pieds might be a further manifestation of the already known Continental Clearflighted, but investigations disproved the suggestion.

The history of the Australian Dominant Pied is a most interesting one, starting with the appearance of a Banded Pied in Sydney, Australia during 1935, which is some few years after the Danish Recessive mutation and a number of years prior to the arrival of the Continental Clearflighted. Reports do not seem to indicate in whose aviaries this Pied mutation appeared, but this bird and its parents (a Sky Blue cock and an Olive Green hen) were bought by Keith Ings who then evolved his Australian Dominant Pied Strain. From the colour of its parents, the original Pied must have been a Dark Green and also split for Blue.

For some time there was much discussion in the Fancy Press both at home and overseas as to the general make-up of the Australian Pieds and their link, if any, with the Danish Pieds and Continental Clearflighted. The various manifestations of the Australian Pieds were attributed to the bird having two, four or six factors (modifiers), each giving a different visual appearance. We now know that the Australian Pied character is a Dominant one and that the distribution of its pattern markings is affected by modifying agents, with some influence derived from distant cross pairings with Danish Recessive Pieds and Continental Clearflighted.

Information in this country about the origin of the Australian Dominant Pieds was first published in an Article in *Cage Birds* that was extracted from the writings of Alex Holmes, Editor of *Bird World, Australia, May 1953. In the Budgerigar Bulletin* of September 1962 H.P. Williams, Secretary of **The Pied Budgerigar Society of Great Britain**, gave confirming details. All the Australian Dominant Pieds in Great Britain today appear to have their origin in two unringed cock birds — a **Pied Grey** and a **Pied Green** bought from a bird dealer's shop in Bristol by A.M. Cooper of Caerleon, South Wales, during 1957/8, whilst the import ban was lifted. The first examples to be seen by the general public in this country were exhibited at the 1958 National Exhibition of *Cage and Aviary Birds*, London, where they aroused considerable interest amongst Budgerigar breeders and exhibitors. Most of the birds shown during the following few seasons were of the Banded Pied type like the original birds and all stemmed from the Cooper strain.

I obtained **Pied Green** birds from A.M. Cooper which proved to be split for Blue with the cocks also split for Opaline. In my correspondence with him I gathered that he had crossed Fallows, Whites, Opalines, Cinnamons, Greywings and Whites, Albinos, Lutinos and Lacewings with his Pieds in an attempt to produce more Pieds per nest. These crosses however did not achieve the hoped for result and only gave Pieds in more variety and often of unsatisfactory colourings. The number of actual Pieds produced from a non Pied and a Dominant Pied worked out overall at 50% of each kind as would be expected from a single character Dominant. My own experiments in those early days using only pure Normal Greens and Blues for crossing also gave a figure of 50%. As with all cross matings individual results varied quite considerably, and this fact did lead some breeders to think they had discovered special crossings to produce more Pieds. The facts mentioned above are supported in Articles by H.P. Williams in the June 1961 and September 1962 Issues of *The Budgerigar Bulletin*.

Some breeders used Recessive Pieds as mates for their Australian Dominant Pieds thinking that two Pied birds although of different mutations would give a better percentage of Pieds. As we now know this was a mistake and only resulted in latter generations of Dominant Pieds actually showing Recessive Pied colour patterns; that is, missing throat spots, broken cheek flashes and loss of dark colour pattern. This breakdown in the Dominant Pied colour pattern can still be seen today in numerous specimens that have been bred from birds 'tainted' with the Recessive Pied character.

Formation of Pied Budgerigar Society

As it can be visualised, the Australian Dominant Pied mutation quickly became popular both on the show benches and breeding aviaries all over the country. Being of a Dominant nature the overall quality of these Australian Pieds quickly developed and soon over-shadowed the slower improving Danish Recessive Pieds. At one time it did seem that the Danish Recessive Pieds might drop into obscurity because of the rapid increase in popularity of the Australian Dominant

Figure 4.4   Ideal Recessive Pied and Ideal Clearflight
From: **Pied Budgerigar Society** pamphlet

Figure 4.5   Ideal Banded Pied and Ideal Dominant Pied.
From: **Pied Budgerigar Society** pamphlet

Pieds. This state of affairs caused a small group of keen Pied enthusiasts to form in August 1959 the first Specialist Budgerigar Society in Great Britain — **The Pied Budgerigar Society of Great Britain** with H.P. Williams as Secretary.

This new Society was somewhat on the lines of the previously formed **Pied Budgerigar Society of Australia**, but this time catering for *all* kinds of Pied mutations. At a meeting held in Birmingham on April 9th, 1960, *Colour Standards* for **Recessive Pieds, Dominant Pieds, Clear-flighted** and **Dark-eyed Clears** were finalised and a pictorial ideal of these Pied varieties adopted. It was initially through the untiring efforts of the officers and committee of the **Pied Budgerigar Society** of Great Britain that the Pied varieties were fully integrated into the Budgerigar world.

This Specialist Society flourished for a number of years and really developed interest in the Pied varieties all over the country and then, owing to administrative difficulties, it began to fade. As this was happening a new Pied Specialist Society came into being in 1960, and was called the **Variegated Budgerigar Club** having its aims based on those originally formulated by the Pied Budgerigar Society.

The basic work in organising the new Society was quietly and efficiently carried by Alan Fullilove who became its first Secretary. In due course the Variegated Budgerigar Club became an Associated Society of **The Budgerigar Society** and together they revised the colour and points *standards* for all the Pied forms. If it had not been for the great efforts, firstly by **The Pied Budgerigar Society of Great Britain** and latterly by **The Variegated Budgerigar Club**, it seems certain that the Recessive Pied mutation would have suffered the same fate as that of the Light Yellows, Fallows and Greywings. At the present time Recessive Pieds are making real headway, but the Continental Clear-flighted and Dark-eyed Clears are very much in the background. As time goes on and with the support from the **Variegated Budgerigar Club** these two now neglected Pied forms can be brought to the fore once again.

Australian Clearflighted Pied

Some time after the Australian Dominant Pied mutation had been developed, a further Pied kind appeared in that country and was called the Australian Clearflighted. These birds did not possess the head spot which is a characteristic of the Australian Pied and it was only their flight feathers, and occasionally central tail feathers, that were clear. As with the Continental Clearflighted, the number of flights that were clear varied from a complete set to only a few feathers in one wing.

The origin of these Clearflighted is not clear, it was said they were developed from the Pieds, or they were a further mutation of the Pieds. When I obtained some of these Australian Clearflights from the English breeder, I was able to carry out a series of experiments, and found they were a separate mutation from other Pied kinds. Although I corresponded numerous discussions with both Australian and New Zealand breeders of these birds, I could not uncover any definite information on their origin.

During the period that A.M. Cooper (1957/8) was developing his Australian Pied strain in Great Britain R.C.F. Dibbins of Reading reported that he had an unusual Clearflighted bird that was unlike the well known Continental type. He had bought this bird from a dealer's mixed batch of Budgerigars because of its colouring. It was thought, and later proved to be correct, that this bird was of Australian origin and most likely had come into this country along with the Cooper birds. My breeding experiments showed that when these birds were crossed with Recessive Pieds they did not ultimately produce Dark-eyed Clears, as if a Continental Clearflight had been used. The only apparent difference that resulted from this cross was the appearance of a head spot, and a slight breaking of the body colouring in some of the Australian Clearflight/Recessive Pied young. I think this point proved conclusively that the two Clear-flighted types were due to separate mutations.

Figure 5.1 A much over-spotted Bird. By accentuating any one feature a breeder can ruin the balance of a bird.

From: *Exhibition Budgerigars* by Dr. M.D.S. Armour

CHAPTER 5

HISTORY OF THE MUTATIONS
III — DEVELOPING THE COLOURS

While the Pied varieties were being established in Britain, other exciting colour mutations were fast appearing.

WHITES, YELLOWS AND ROYAL BLUES

In Britain, breeders were concentrating on improving **Whites** and **Yellows of deep suffusion**, the ultimate aim being to produce birds that were clear yellow or white on head, neck, back and wings, with a very dark body colour. Our breeders met with some success and a number of handsome looking birds were bred and exhibited.

French breeders were also breeding on similar lines, but mainly with Yellows of deep suffusion, and their efforts produced birds with about 60% of normal body colour with very lightly marked yellow wings. These birds went under the name of **Goldwings** and were said, at the time, to be the same as Australian birds of similar type now being developed. I imported three pairs of these Goldwings from France and found them to be just a little better in colour than the best of our own Yellows of deep suffusion. Their wing colour was deeper yellow, with only very pale markings, and their body colour was about the same depth but much more brilliant.

At the same time, British Budgerigar breeders learned of the arrival in this country of a pair or Royal Blue Budgerigars. This news was given as follows in *Budgerigar Bulletin* No. 30, June 1934:

Some time ago a pair of these birds were presented to His Majesty the King by Mr. Harold E. Peir of Peakhurst, Sydney, New South Wales, and we have the honour of receiving permission from Sir Clive Wigram, Private Secretary to the King, to publish a copy of the following letter with regards to these birds:-

83

The "Royal Blue" Budgerigars

'The birds are classified as Greywing Cobalts and the strain is popularly known as Royal Blues. The donor and breeder, Mr. Harold E. Peir of Peakhurst, New South Wales, is one of the foremost breeders in Australia, and has produced every known variety of these birds.

Mr Peir has definitely established a strain of birds with pure cobalt blue body colour, and is at present experimenting in the production of a strain of bi-coloured birds possessing the same intensity of body colour but with white wings and upper parts.

He states that the period occupied in producing and establishing his Royal Blue strain of Budgerigars was seven years.'

(signed) Neville Cayley, Chair,
The Budgerigar Club of New South Wales.

AUSTRALIAN MUTATIONS — THE CLEARWING

In the March 1933 *Budgerigar Bulletin* No. 24 Dr. Merrilees of Australia made some interesting observations on Budgerigar culture in his country. It would seem Dr. Merrilees wrote that before the ban on the export and import of Australian birds, most of the Australian breeders' aviaries were stocked with birds derived from Japanese stock. This is an interesting fact, as we know that the bulk of the Japanese Budgerigars came from Europe and Great Britain in particular. On looking back it will be found that quite a lot of the colour mutations first appeared in Australia, where the stock, according to Dr. Merrilees, was made up of a good mixture of birds of Japanese origin.

The first information published that a new mutation may have occurred in Australia was in the June 1933 *Budgerigar Bulletin* No. 25. It was given under "News from our Australian Members":

Our keen Australian members are interested in the variation of suffusions of Budgerigars, such as are known to exist ... At the April meeting of the Victorian Budgerigar Society a paper was read on this subject, and a number of Greywings were exhibited to illustrate the variation in the depth of suffusion on the body and depth of grey on the wings and flights ... It is however of great interest to read that they also exhibited at this meeting Greywings and other birds which seemed to hold out hopes that Australia may give us two new varieties; (a) Birds with very dark or normal bodies, but very lightly marked, or even ultimately, white wings. (b) Birds with very light or even white or yellow bodies, but very deep grey or even normal black wings.

From reading this, it is certain that some of the 'Greywings' must have had what we now know as the Clearwing character, either being actual Clearwings (the birds with the palest wings) or Full Body Coloured Greywings (the birds with grey wings and a hard and brilliant body colour). From these scant particulars that were available at the time it is difficult to say which came first, the Full Body Coloured Greywings or the Clearwings. We are now fully aware that **Greywing, Clearwing** and **Dilute** are separate mutations of the same gene and form what is known as a multiple allelomorph.

There was much discussion amongst breeders, and many articles and letters appeared in the Fancy Press both at home and overseas about the possibilities of a new mutation. After examining all the available documentary evidence it became clear that the Australian Clearwing mutation could not have occurred later than about 1932. Most probably the original mutation happened some few years earlier but was not identified as such because of the presence of the Greywing character at the same time.

In the *Budgerigar Bulletin* No. 30, June 1934, comes further information of the existence of Clearwings, in an article by S.E. Terrell of Adelaide, South Australia, on nomenclature of Budgerigars. He said that **Normal Yellows** and **Normal Silvers** (Whites) were not generally known . . . Lightwings exist in the old familiar yellows, light, medium and dark. Also in Australia in greens, light, medium and dark. This I have always taken to mean that in addition to the Yellows, which of course have light wings, there were green coloured birds also with light wings — the Clearwings.

The Austral Factor, Yellow-wings and Whitewings

Writing in the June 1935 *Budgerigar Bulletin* No. 34, on naming Budgerigar colours, S.E. Terrell said that the colour in these deep body coloured birds was due to a new factor (character) — the Austral factor and gave **Austral Greens** in three shades and Royal or **Austral Blues** also in three shades. Another writer, J.S. Thonemann of Melbourne, Australia, gives credit to H.E. Peir for first producing **Yellow-wings** and **Whitewings.** Undoubtedly these birds were bred through his Royal Blue strain as sent to His Majesty King George V. The first colour plates of birds having the "Austral" factor were published in *Budgerigars in Bush and Aviary* by Neville W. Cayley, F.R.Z.S. in 1933.

It will now have been realised that although much has been written about this new colour character there was still a variance in naming the birds and their genetical scheme was uncertain. However, in the March 1936 *Budgerigar Bulletin* No. 37 an Australian correspondent wrote:

> The yellow-wing green has been said to be only a yellow bred by selection to a really green body colour and still retaining the yellow wing. This is not so, as it is definitely a separate mutation and is recessive only to normal green, and when split white will produce the white-wing blues as well as yellow-wing greens, ordinary yellows, and ordinary whites. The greywings we have with full depth of body colour (100%) are merely true greywings crossed with these yellow-wings or whitewings.

In the following Issue, I wrote an article on suffusions, supported by breeding results from thirty-one different matings, showing that suffusion could only be increased to a certain limit and that Clearwings could not be bred by selection from these deeply suffused birds. It should be remembered that up to that time live Yellow-wings and Whitewings had not been seen by fanciers in this country.

Later in that year (1936) a consignment of Whitewings and Yellow-wings were brought to this country by E. Walker of Sydney, Australia, for three Midland Budgerigar breeders, Messrs. Mott, Marshall and Birch. All these fanciers were successful in reproducing Clearwings in this country before further importations were made.

The following information on some of these birds is contained in a letter I received from P.A. Birch in July 1938. He wrote:

> ... in September 1936 I imported in conjunction with Messrs. Mott and Marshall one pair of Whitewing Cobalts from Australia. I had one round from these birds almost at once and produced three Whitewing Cobalts, unfortunately during the winter the hen died. I thought the original birds were split White, but the following breeding record seems to prove otherwise.
>
> In 1937 the imported cock paired to a Light Yellow/White produced two Yellow-wing Light Greens, one Yellow-wing Dark Green and two Whitewing Cobalts, the young birds bred in 1936 produced Clearwings when paired to Yellows and Whites in addition to a few Yellows and Whites.
>
> This year (1938) I paired the old cock to a White Cobalt hen and they produced eight Whitewing Cobalts, four Whitewing Mauves and one Whitewing Sky Blue ... These birds are all outstanding in size and type but there seems to be a lot of variation in the purity of the wing colour even from birds in the same nest.

I saw these birds and was amazed at the wonderful depth of body colour and the purity of the wings in some specimens, and they were certainly quite different from any deeply suffused Yellows or Whites we had here. However it was not until the June 1937 Budgerigar Bulletin No. 42 that the first full explanation of **Yellow-wings, Whitewings,** and **Australs** was given by R.B. Browne of Hornsby, New South Wales, showing their colour was caused by a mutant factor and not by selective breeding as often thought. In his Article R.B. Browne gave genetical formula for all these birds and this received the full agreement of Professor F.A.E. Crew.

Breeding and Showing Developments

For the next few years the breeding of Clearwings, as the Group was now called, went strongly ahead and there were some truly beautifully coloured specimens produced by their numerous keen breeders. At most of the larger shows Clearwing classes received very big entries and competition amongst breeders was extremely keen and the group seemed set for a fine future. Many birds were being bred with 85% to 95% of normal body colour with light areas of wings and so on, almost clear yellow or clear white.

Unfortunately this was not to be as the 1939-45 War period saw the decline of many of the Colour Mutations of Budgerigars, including the Clearwings. As it would be expected, breeding stocks of Clearwings were very low but this did not deter a few dedicated breeders and slowly but surely the numbers of Yellow-wings and Whitewings did begin to increase. At the National Exhibition of Cage and Aviary Birds held on December 7th 1963 a number of Clearwing breeders met and formed the **Clearwing Budgerigar Breeders Association** under the Chairmanship of the late S.V.A. Parsons with his son S.D. Parsons as Secretary. The formation of this Specialist Society was the beginning of the Clearwing new rise to popularity, both as aviary and exhibition birds. This can be substantiated by the fact that at their Club Show, held in conjunction with the Budgerigar Society's Silver Jubilee Club Show in November 1977 at the Grandby Halls, Leicester, the entries in the Clearwing classes were 560 out of a total of 4888. This is I think the largest number of a single variety benched at one show and certainly the greatest gathering of Clearwings ever seen.

OPALINE

Following closely on the heels of the Australian Clearwing mutation came the Opaline, which seems to have appeared at approximately the same time in Australia, Europe and Great Britain.

Australian Opaline

In the September 1936 *Budgerigar Bulletin* No. 39, S.E. Terrell of Adelaide, Australia, gave an account of a new mutation that had first been mentioned in the previous Bulletin. These notes have been extracted from S.E. Terrell's excellent article:

> . . . **As we now have nine specimens of the new variety, representing three generations, and belonging to three separate colour classes, we feel justified in making the announcement . . . The new mutant was discovered amongst thousands of wild budgerigars that had been sent to the Adelaide market by trappers. She was a hen bird in juvenile plumage, though that fact was not apparent at the time because the juvenile Light greens of the new variety have brilliant coloured plumage, totally devoid of the dullness usually associated with nestling plumage. Mr. R.J. Byfield of Hobart, Tasmania, was shown a young bird in nestling plumage, and was struck by the vividness of the colours. When asked if he could suggest a name for the new variety, he immediately suggested opalines . . . The original mutant proved to be a very shy and unreliable breeder. Her first year's progeny amounted to three cocks and one hen, the first of which was hatched in August 1934, when she was about two years old. They were all normal greens in appearance, their father being a blue silver (White Sky Blue). When they were about fifteen months old, the three sons were mated up. One was mated to a normal cobalt hen and one with a cinnamon light green hen. These matings produced a total of six opalines, all hens. One is an opaline cobalt, and**

the remainder are opaline light greens and opaline dark greens.

The third son was mated with his mother and has produced at least three opalines, two of which (a cock and a hen) are out of the nest, and the third had quill feathers just sufficiently advanced to show that it is an opaline. Another younger one is as yet uncertain, which looks like an opaline . . . One of the young (opaline) cocks mated to a normal hen produced an opaline, we therefore concluded, as soon as the colour variations were discernible in the quill feathers, that the new factor must be a sex-linked one, and that the young opaline must turn out to be a hen . . .

This article was written in 1936 and it states therein that there were now three generations of Opalines in Australia which seems to indicate that the original mutant Light Green hen was hatched some time in 1932. A comparison between the normal Budgerigar markings and the new Opaline pattern markings is clearly shown in the photograph that accompanied the article.

As soon as stock became available examples of the Australian Opaline mutation were imported into Great Britain in 1937. The first to come was an Opaline Green cock which arrived at H. Tod Boyd's, London, aviaries during the summer of that year, and I reported this fact in my notes in *Bird Fancy*. I had the opportunity of seeing this bird soon after he arrived and was immediately struck by his **vivid colouring** throughout. The undulations on head and neck were very light on a bright yellow ground, the mantle area clear, the wing undulations wide and heavily suffused with the mantle colour. There was a distinct wide light bar visible on the outer primaries and the two long central tail feathers had a dark shaft surrounded by a light area edged with dark blue. The mask was ornamented with six medium sized round black spots quite free from flecks, ticks or extra spots.

British-bred Opaline

Prior to this information on the Australian Opaline mutation, a further mutation had occurred in Scotland and was known first as **Pied** or Piebald and later as **Marbled.** This news was given in a short article in the September 1935 *Budgerigar Bulletin* No. 35. I quote:

Mr. R.G. Ashby reports that Mrs. Ashby has produced three freaks from the mating of a pied cobalt hen with its son. The pied cobalt hen has cobalt markings instead of white and all three of the young, which are two cocks and a hen are marked similarly to their mother . . . The history of this case is that two years ago (1933), Mrs. Ashby obtained a cobalt hen with exceptional throat spots and freakish markings being bred from a normal Mauve and a Sky Blue by A. Brown of Kilmarnock . . . Breeding it with one of her best light green cocks, one which was believed to be pure green. The mating produced sky blues, light greens and a dark green, this proved the cock was not pure but split blue. It was one of these sky blue cocks mated to his mother that produced the three further Pieds . . .

This original **Opaline Cobalt** hen was quite a good, reliable breeder and in due time gave a considerable number of young with all the cocks carrying the new character. Within a few seasons quantities of the birds, now officially called Opalines, were in the hands of several British breeders; in addition Mrs. Ashby, W.E. Higham, F.Z.S.., M.B.O.U. (then President of the **Budgerigar Society**) were carrying out experiments with this strain. In an Article in the December 1936 *Budgerigar Bulletin* No.40 W.E. Higham gave his breeding results which clearly indicated that the mutation was sex-linked and of the same colouring as the Australian mutation. He also mentioned that these Opalines had very large throat spots, which often covered most of the mask, and thought it was a peculiarity of the strain. We know today that it certainly was, as multiplicity of throat spots is very troublesome in many of our stocks. Photographs accompanying W.E. Higham's article depicted three examples showing their markings clearly, and that they were akin to those of the Australian mutation.

Continental Opaline

Whilst the Opalines were being developed in Australia and Great Britain, news was trickling through from Europe that yet a further Opaline mutation had occurred there at about the same time. In spite of exhaustive enquiries the exact location of this mutation was not forthcoming, some said Belgium or Holland and others Germany, but nothing definite. The Continental bird books do not give any clue, but the mutation certainly happened, with the first examples coming to Great Britain in 1937.

I saw specimens of these European Opalines soon after they arrived and they were similarly coloured to the Australian birds, only their overall colouring was far less bright and certainly not as rich. They had, however, very fine sets of round, well-spaced, black throat spots which were absent in the British strain. I mentioned about these Continental Opalines in my Notes in the August 1937 Issue of *Bird Fancy* after I had seen birds imported by W.E. Higham and others. This now made three widely separated appearances of a mutation having the same hereditary characters, and their blending together over the years has resulted in our present-day strains of Opalines.

Breeding the Mutation

It has now been ascertained that the Australian Opaline mutation occurred in 1932, the Scottish in 1934, and the Continental about the same time. Whilst looking over some old documents in preparation for this book I came across a most interesting letter dated 4th April 1940. The contents had slipped my memory completely and I have not seen them mentioned anywhere else. It was from W.K. Cox of Olton, Birmingham, a very well known breeder and exhibitor of Budgerigars of that period. He wrote:

> With reference to Opalines, I herewith have pleasure in forwarding you the
> details of which I think were the first English mutation. It was in May 1933 that
> Mr. Marriott of Wolverhampton discovered an unusual coloured youngster in
> the nest, which turned out to be an Opaline Greywing Green hen ... It was shown
> at Wolverhampton Open Show later that year and gained a first in the A.O.C.
> class, although the Judge or no one else knew just what colour she was ... Mr.
> Marriott was very much sought after by interested fanciers who wished to
> purchase the bird and he finally decided to let me have her to see what I could do
> with it. I first enquired what it was bred from and was told that Mr. Marriott
> bought a cheap cock which he thought was a Yellow/White and paired it to a
> Greywing Blue hen. The young produced in the first nest were five hens, four
> Greywing Light Greens and the Opaline Greywing Green which was passed on to
> me. I paired the Opaline Greywing Green hen to a White Sky Blue cock and in two
> rounds produced three Greywing Green cocks and five Greywing Green hens.
> Unfortunately the Opaline hen died before any other pairing could be made, this
> left me still in the dark. So next year I paired the three Greywing Green cocks to
> three Greywing Green hens, they were sisters to the first Opaline which Mr.
> Marriott had forwarded to me. All the young produced were again Greywing
> Greens which seemed to be hopeless. However I had another go by pairing the
> Greywing Green cocks (which were split for Opaline) to Cinnamon White hens,
> and out of one nest I got an Opaline Green hen. Now I was convinced that I had a
> sex-linked variety ... I paired all the cock birds I had bred from this strain to
> Whites and Cinnamon Whites and produced Opaline Greywing Blue hens and
> Opaline Greywing Green hens. I have paired these hens to various split cocks and
> have produced Opaline cocks and hens in Blue, Cobalt, Green and Yellow ...

It will be seen from the above letter that Mr. Marriott's original
Opaline Greywing Green hen was bred from a Yellow/White cock of
unknown pedigree. From this it can be assumed that this cock bird was
carrying the Opaline character in split form and that the mutation
probably occurred during 1932, a year before the Opaline hen
appeared. I do not know just what happened to this particular Opaline
mutation as it was during the beginning of the Second World War
period that it was starting to be developed in many different colours. It is
feasible that some of these Opalines were incorporated in with the three
other existing Opaline mutations, thereby contributing to our present
day Opaline strain.

The original Opaline Greywing Green hen must have been the first to
appear in Great Britain and certainly the first to be exhibited. Opalines
in many colour varieties now rank amongst the most popular of all the
different kinds of Budgerigars. It is rather sad I think that only very few
of the thousands of Opalines bred each year show the lovely pattern and
brilliant colour the original Australian mutation possessed.

GREY BUDGERIGARS

The first mention of a "Grey" mutation was made by F.S. Elliott in
the March 1935 *Budgerigar Bulletin* No. 33, where he reported that H.T.

Watson of Bedford had in his possession a hen of a slatey blue colour. This hen in adult plumage had been bought from a dealer in August 1933, but he could not obtain any particulars of its parentage. The bird was paired with a White Cobalt cock and they raised two normally coloured cobalt young — a cock and a hen. The old hen, unfortunately, died before any further offspring could be obtained and H.T. Watson kindly sent me the skin of this bird which I had in my possession for many years until it disintegrated.

The two young Cobalts were paired together but there is no record of any "Grey" birds being produced from them before they died. Some years ago before this skin deteriorated and fell to pieces, I compared it with some live specimens of **Slate Cobalts** I had at the time and the colours were identical. This likeness of colour made me conclude that the Watson "Grey" was in fact a Slate Cobalt and although it was no doubt the first Slate to appear in Great Britain she was not the first Grey.

Recessive Greys

The next breeding of Grey Budgerigars in Great Britain is recorded in a letter from E.W. Brooks of Mitcham, Surrey, in the June 1935 *Budgerigar Bulletin* No. 34. He wrote:

> . . . last year (1933) I bred three grey birds, all from a Cobalt mating — two hens from the first round and a cock from the second. I hope to mate the cock to one of the hens.

Further information about these birds was given by E.W. Brooks and myself in *Cage Birds, Bird Fancy* and in the September 1935 *Budgerigar Bulletin* No. 35. In a letter to me dated October 17th 1937 Mr. Brooks reported that he had now bred these Grey birds in a number of different varieties and depths of colour, including both White and Yellow specimens. He also said that the Greys were a definite mutation and that they were Recessive in their behaviour.

I saw the first **Grey Yellows** in the nest when nearly feathered and was struck by their very dark mustard yellow body colour. It also appeared that these Grey birds were not very strong and it took some time to develop and breed them in fair numbers. The darkest specimens were the Recessive Grey form of the **Mauve** and such birds appeared to be almost black grey, the nearest to black that has been bred up to that time and since.

The body colour in all three depths of shade were far deeper than the now well known Australian Dominant Greys with the **Recessive Grey Blue** being as deep in colour as the **Dominant Grey Mauve.** The markings and long central tail feathers in all these Recessive Greys were a solid dull black and even the cheek flashes were dull grey. Only a few fanciers other than E.W. Brooks had these Greys, but an odd example or two were exhibited. Unfortunately, before the strain became more widely distributed amongst breeders, the **Dominant Australian Greys** appeared on the scene and the Recessive Greys became even fewer in number. During the Second World War period this Recessive mutation was lost and has not, as far as records indicate, reappeared again here or elsewhere.

Dominant Australian Greys

In the *Budgerigar Bulletin* of September 1935 No. 35 there was a letter from a Mrs. S. Harrison of Murrumbeena, Australia, giving news of a further Grey mutation:

> **Referring to your article on Grey Budgerigars, last year I obtained a definitely grey cock, pedigree unknown, from a dealer and I mated it with a common light green. The result was: 1 grey cock, 1 cobalt cock. I next mated the grey cock with a white blue hen and first round produced: 1 grey cock, 1 grey hen, 1 sky blue hen, 1 cobalt hen. The next round gave: 1 grey cock, 1 white grey hen, 1 cobalt hen, 1 white blue hen. Thus you will see that the results are quite different from what I would have obtained from a mauve cock . . . I have kept the young grey cock from the grey x green mating, also the grey hen from the second mating and I have mated them both with olives, while the original grey cock is mated to another white blue hen. If there are any greys from these pairs, you will see that I shall then have three generations of greys.**

These results show that the original common Light Green hen was split for Blue and a further mating of the Grey cock indicated that he was split for White. The following Bulletin contained further articles on both the Brooks and Harrison Greys together with some more interesting breeding results. From this information it was quite evident that the Brooks mutation was a Recessive one and darker overall in colour than the Dominant Harrison mutation.

During the next few months much was written about the Grey birds in the Fancy Press both at home and overseas, and Fanciers discussed at great length the possibilities of these new birds. In the March 1936 *Budgerigar Bulletin* No. 37 it was reported that further Grey birds had been discovered in Australia. W.F. Shepherd of Kew, Victoria, Australia, wrote saying that he had some Grey Budgerigars that were identical in every way to those being bred by Mrs. Harrison and promised to send further information.

It is interesting to note that in the same *Bulletin* it was reported that the use of **coloured closed year dated metal rings** had been approved for use by the Council of **The Budgerigar Society**. Today we take the use of these rings as normal but in those early days there was much discussion between Fanciers as to the relative values of the plain and the coloured metal rings. A further interesting and important event took place during 1935, when Professor F.A.E. Crew and Rowena Lamy of the Institute of Animal Genetics, Edinburgh University, published a book *The Genetics of the Budgerigar*, which explained just how the different mutations were inherited and why. This work was a major contribution to the knowledge of colour breeding of Budgerigars.

More news about the Grey variety was contained in the June *Budgerigar Bulletin* No. 38 of 1936; W.F. Shepherd gave further details of the breeding of his Grey birds and there was also a note from Germany reporting further Greys. W.F. Shepherd wrote:

> The grey birds I was lucky enough to procure came from a flock (colony) breeder who had in his aviaries only greywings, and although I have been visiting his place constantly since I had the birds, I have been unable to locate the parents. At present I have two grey hens, one grey cock and one grey green hen. Speaking now of the grey green the general body colour and colour of the lower back, rump and breast, flanks and underparts are a pure clear olive, absolutely free from flecking or trace of green . . . I have had the privilege of judging Mrs. Harrison's greys on the bench and also examining them at close quarters in her aviaries, and she has also seen mine. We mutually agree that there are three shades, viz: light, medium and dark grey. On comparison we came to the conclusion that my birds are of the light grey variety.

This information makes it certain that the Shepherd Greys are a similar mutation in all respects to the ones evolved by Mrs. Harrison. Both groups of these Greys came on the scene at approximately the same time in widely separated parts of Australia. It can therefore be assumed they were each due to a separate mutation. A report in the German *Budgerigar* magazine *Der Wellensittich* of March 1936 said that Karl Feyh of Chemmitz had bred, from a pair of Sky Blues, one Grey in the first round and a further one in the second. Although no further information seems available about this German Grey mutation, I gathered from correspondence that a strain was established.

It was in the middle of 1937 that Walter E. Higham obtained his first Australian Grey from Mrs. Harrison, Australia — a fine cock bird. Shortly after this several other fanciers, including myself, imported Greys from Mrs. Harrison. My birds were Grey Greens split for Blue and one cock bird was split for Opaline as well.

Being of a Dominant nature of inheritance the Australian Greys quickly increased in numbers and were soon finding favour with a large number of breeders. The ease with which Australian Greys could be reproduced had a drastic effect on the English Greys, and the Australian Grey Greens had an adverse effect on the breeding of Olive Greens from which they have never recovered. As it will be realised the Australian Grey forms of all the other varieties were soon being bred and many combinations quickly found their way on to the show benches.

Over the past few years Greys (Grey Greens) have dominated the exhibition field in their Normal, Opaline and Cinnamon forms, many times winning Best Budgerigar in Show at all major exhibitions including the National and Budgerigar Society Club Shows. The Greys (Grey Greens) are likely to hold their popularity for some time to come, although there is now a tendency for other mutations to start a comeback in some areas of the country.

SLATE BUDGERIGARS

It will have been seen from the above that Australian Dominant Grey Budgerigars did not actually reach Great Britain until 1937. Before they arrived another mutation of a somewhat similar colour had appeared in the aviaries of T.S. Bowman of Carlisle and examples were actually exhibited here in 1935. Extracts from an article by the original breeder, which appeared in the *Budgerigar Bulletin* No. 38 of June 1936 give the history of this British mutation.

> I bred the first Slate Budgerigar in May 1935 and it was bred under control from a Cobalt cock and a Sky Blue hen. The cock was one of my own breeding and hatched in early July 1934 from a Cobalt cock and a Mauve hen; the Sky Blue hen's pedigree was unknown ... my records show that the first round hatched in May 1935 consisted of two hens one Cobalt and one Slate. In the second round in June I had three Cobalt cocks and another Slate hen ... I exhibited a Slate hen in the A.O.C. class at Dumfries on 23rd November 1935 and was placed 4th, a little later the same bird was placed 2nd at Bradford and highly commended at the Crystal Palace ... they differ in their colouring and breeding behaviour from the Greys of Mrs. Harrison and Mr. Brooks which are Dominant and Recessive respectively whereas my birds I am sure are Sex-linked.

T.S. Bowman's breeding results the following year gave further Slates including a cock from the original Cobalt and his Slate daughter. Slate hens were also bred from some of the male nest mates of the Slate hens when paired to Normal hens. From these results it can be concluded that the mutation in the first place was on one of the X chromosome pair of the original Cobalt cock. This is shown by the fact that he consistently produced Slate hens and some of his male offspring have done likewise. When paired to one of his daughters Slate cocks resulted, confirming that the mutation was a Sex-linked one.

Coloration

As their numbers slowly increased, it became clear that there could be a Slate form of all other existing varieties in three depths of shade in both the **Green and Blue series**. The name Slate given to these birds in the first case by T.S. Bowman was an apt one as it described their body colour extremely accurately. The name Slate was in due course adopted by **The Budgerigar Society**. Their wing markings are very clear cut black on white with dull deep blue long central tail feathers and cheek patches of dull violet. Their body colour shows a slight bluish undertone and is quite distinct from the pure level clear grey shade of the Dominant Greys. The most outstanding difference between this mutation and the Greys is that the latter have black long central tail feathers with no trace whatsoever of blue. The **Slate Cobalts** are a deeper slate shade with rather a warmer tone and the **Slate Mauve** are very deep, being the darkest of all the Budgerigar colours. Like the Greys the body colours are solid all through without flecking or breaks of other shades.

For a time Slates were being bred by a few interested colour breeders but they never caught on as exhibition birds, mainly I feel due to the appearance of the easier to breed Australian Dominant Greys. The most interesting Slate form to be bred in these earlier days was I think a **Slate Cinnamon White Blue** hen that was raised in the aviaries of W.G. Roderick of Purley, Surrey. She was in actual fact a White of deep suffusion and her slate suffusion could be clearly seen, even though it was softened and diluted somewhat by the Cinnamon character. As far as I have been able to trace she is the only example of this particular combination to have been bred.

Breeding and Exhibiting

The fact that the Slate character is **sex-linked** undoubtedly saved it from extinction during the War period, as it was passed on mainly in split form during that time. In the late 1950's and early 1960's a few colour breeders, including myself, made an attempt to revive an interest in breeding and exhibiting Slates. We met with some success in their breeding, but as most of the Slates then available were of the Opaline form it took several seasons before the Normal and then further varieties could be produced. Slates were bred in **Yellow-face Blue and Cobalt, Cobalt, Greywing Blue, Dominant Pied Blue and Cobalt, Recessive Pied Blue, Cobalt, Mauve and Yellow-face Cobalt** and a few examples of the **Green** series. I was also fortunate in breeding several **Continental Clear-flighted** Slates with one hen being the most perfectly marked specimen of that variety I have ever produced.

In spite of these efforts Slates did not gain much ground, although today they are still being bred and even exhibited in small numbers from time to time. My own aviaries have recently produced a Recessive Pied Slate Blue hen and a Slate Blue hen; Slates will probably be with us, in limited numbers, for a long time to come. Incidentally, the first actual Slate to be bred and noted in this country was the so-called Watson 'Grey' in 1933 (see account on page 90).

Figure 6.1 Young Hen with excessive Feathering. Her shape is ruined by the body feather dangling round her feet and vent.
From: *Exhibition Budgerigars* by Dr. M.D.S. Armour

CHAPTER 6

HISTORY OF THE MUTATIONS
IV — DEVELOPMENTS SINCE 1930's

During the 1930's colour mutations amongst the domesticated Budgerigar population were, as indicated, quite considerable with the number of possible colour forms being very much extended. This was not the end of the expansion however.

YELLOW-FACED BIRDS

In *Budgerigar Bulletin* No. 39 of June 1936 and also in the Fancy Press a further new variety was recorded under the names of **Golden Cobalts, Yellow masked or Yellow faced.** These birds were first reported by two breeders, Mrs. G. Lait of Grimsby and Jack Long of Gorleston-on-Sea, both having bred Blue birds with yellow masks. Mrs. Lait's first Yellow masked bird was a Greywing Mauve hen bred from a Dark Green/White cock paired to a Greywing Mauve hen, whereas Jack Long's three Yellow masked birds were Cobalt cocks. These cocks were bred from a Dark Green cock and what was then described as a 'Green' hen having a heavy turquoise suffusion on breast, flanks and rump. In the light of present day knowledge this 'Green' hen was undoubtedly an actual Yellow-faced bird herself, as no Normal Blue birds appeared amongst her young by a Dark Green/Blue cock. This fact puts the appearance of this Yellow-faced form back to at least 1935.

It was also discovered that Yellow-faced birds had been breeding in a small aviary on the Norfolk coast for a number of years without the owner being aware of the fact. To my mind it is very possible that the 'Green' hen that was the founder of Jack Long's strain came from these Norfolk birds, as they both belonged to the same genetical group (Type II) and the distance between the two aviaries was quite short.

It can well be imagined the excitement caused amongst Budgerigar

97

breeders by the appearance of these birds that showed both yellow (green) and blue in their colouring, which had previously been thought to be an impossibility. Various theories were advanced as to the cause of this colour phenomenon and finally it was agreed that their colour was due to a new mutation. A surprising fact was that all the Yellow-faced birds, as they were now officially called, had yellow masks and blue bodies when in nest feather, and when some became adult their plumage gained a greenish over-lay.

Later, after some investigation of numerous breeding results and the study of adult colouring, the conclusion reached was that not one but two separate mutations existed, each showing a somewhat similar colour pattern. In due course, those blue coloured birds showing a yellow mask and a slight yellow suffusion on tail and wing butts became known as **Yellow-faced Blues Type I**. The other kind having a deeper yellow on their mask and a very heavy suffusion of yellow on body, wings and tail were called **Yellow-faced Blues Type II**. To add to the confusion in distinguishing the patterns of breeding behaviour, was the fact that both kinds had been unknowingly crossed together, and a number of birds produced had both of the new characters in their genetical makeup.

The problem of Yellow-faced inheritance persisted for a long time, in fact until the early part of 1960 when a combined attempt to solve the mystery was made by a group of interested colour breeders including Professor G.T. Taylor, Cyril Warner, Matthew Bender (U.S.A.), John Papin (U.S.A.) and myself.

Reproduction methods

I have just mentioned that the difference between Yellow-face Blue Type I and Yellow-face Blue Type II could be detected visually but, in addition, there is a variation in their method of reproduction, which was not apparent for some years. When Yellow-faced Blues were being bred in considerable numbers, reports began to circulate amongst breeders that the percentages of Yellow-faced Blues bred did not conform to the usual Mendelian expectations; for instance, when two Yellow-faced Blues Type I were paired together they gave only 50% Yellow-faced young, the same result as when paired to a Normal Blue. Furthermore some pairs of what looked like Normal Blues were giving all Yellow-faced Blue young, making it appear they were new Yellow-face mutations.

This strange breeding procedure of the Yellow-faced Blue Type I made breeders who were interested in genetics have a closer look at controlled breeding results and to examine and test progeny of such pairings. It was then discovered that amongst the Blues bred from two

Yellow-faced Blue parents were some birds with a special genetical formula. These birds were in fact carrying a double character for Yellow-faced Blue Type I even though they were, in appearance, identical to pure Normal Blues. This revelation put the genetical expectations of Yellow-faced Blue Type I in line with all the other Mendelian calculations. It was also found that because of their position on the chromosomes it was not possible for Green series birds to be split for both Yellow-faced Blue and Normal Blue at the same time. This meant that birds bred from a single character Yellow-faced Blue Type I paired to a Green produced either Green/Blue or Green/Yellow-faced Blue Type I young. There is, of course, no visual difference between these two genetically different green-coloured birds.

Further Mutations

Since the first Yellow-face Blue mutations were recorded in Great Britain a number of others appeared both here and in aviaries in other countries, including at least two kinds with a very deep golden yellow mask, commonly known as **Golden-faced Blues**. In the April 10th, 1937, Issue of *Bird Fancy* a **Yellow-faced White** mutation was recorded as being bred and established in Australia and, in the same Issue, a further British mutation appeared in the aviaries of E.H. Stevenson of Cambridge.

The original Stevenson mutation was a Cobalt cock and had not been used for breeding until his third season. I saw and examined this bird which was quite normal in appearance, although, when paired to several unrelated normal blue coloured hens it produced Yellow-faced Blue and Normal Blue cocks and hens in about equal numbers. Later this mutation was proved to belong to the Type I group.

Exhibiting

Amongst the first exhibitors of the Yellow-faced Blue series were Mrs. Lait, J. Long, F.R. Waite, E.H. Stevenson, W.E. Higham, T.C. Charlton and myself. At the present time the most popular are the Golden-faced and Yellow-faced forms of composite birds mostly known as Rainbows because of their mixture of beautiful vivid colours. It is by combining in one bird the Yellow-face (Golden-face), Opaline and the Clearwing mutations, that the **Yellow-faced (Golden-faced) Opaline Whitewings,** Rainbows, are produced.

In recent years, a great deal of experimental work in sorting out the breeding behaviours of the Golden-faced, Yellow-faced and their combinations has been carried out by K.H. Gray of Tiptree, Essex. He has been able to prove by test pairings that one kind of Golden-faced birds having a single character showed a heavy, deep yellow suffusion all over, whereas when they possessed a double quantity of the Golden-faced character the golden yellow shade was confined to the facial area, wing butts and tail. All the Yellow-faced and Golden-faced mutations have, from time to time, been crossed together giving a big variation in colour shades and, of course, genetical make–up. For many years now he has been the main exhibitor at the **National Exhibition** of good coloured examples of both the Golden-faced and Yellow-faced Rainbows.

VIOLETS

In the 1930's the most favoured colour of all the existing varieties was undoubtedly the Cobalt, and a great many delightfully coloured birds were produced by enthusiastic breeders and exhibitors. At that time rumours began to circulate throughout the Budgerigar Fancy of the appearance of some beautifully coloured Cobalts having a strong violet tone. A few of these specimens were actually exhibited in Cobalt classes and were much admired for their vivid colouring. These specially coloured Cobalts were being bred in Great Britain, Europe and Australia, and it was some time before it was realised that these birds were actually something new. Investigations and experiments were carried out and it was found that these birds were the result of definite mutations and they were given the name of Violet — a very appropriate one too.

As far as I have been able to trace from available literature, there are no definite records stating when or where the first Violet mutation actually occurred. It is known that Violets were mentioned as being bred in several countries from the 1930's to the 1940's. The first documentary evidence of Violets as a new mutation being bred in Great Britain is a list of breeding results and some feathers I have from E.H. Stevenson of Cambridge and H.C. Tucker of Spalding. There is also a letter from Professor F.A.E. Crew of The Institute of Animal Genetics, Edinburgh, giving his opinion on the above-mentioned breeding results. These breeding results cover the years 1936-1938 and the first two initial Violet cocks quoted were wearing 1933 closed coded Budgerigar Society rings. This means that this particular Violet mutation must have occurred not later than 1932.

In his letter the Professor writes:

I have studied the results of your Violet matings carefully and think them quite significant. It seems clear for one thing that *all* **the Violets used were heterozygous for the Violet factor, therefore it must be a Dominant . . . Secondly, your results show that the Violet factor is independent of Dark. A Violet may be genetically Sky Blue, Cobalt or Mauve . . .**

100

This letter is dated May 3rd 1939.

This opinion given by Professor Crew was the correct one and the breeding of Violets today follow his line of thought. Violet is undoubtedly an independent dominant character and is only expressed as a true violet shade when combined with Blue and a single Dark character. When the Violet character is carried by Green series birds it causes them to have an altered shade of colour without any violet showing. Although the fact of Green birds actually possessing the Violet character in their genetical make-up was voiced by Professor Crew, Professor Taylor, Cyril Warner, E.W. Brooks and myself, it was some time before this was accepted by Budgerigar breeders generally.

Exhibition

For a period between the late 1920's, and well into the 1930's Violets, or as they were by them popularly called, **Visual Violet**, to distinguish them from other birds that had the Violet character, were bred quite extensively, and many beautifully coloured Visual Violet birds in different varieties were to be seen on the show benches. It was in 1946-7 that Violets were first given separate classes at the big National Shows and for a time they received excellent support. Later on their popularity waned and they were then exhibited together with other Blue series birds, as they mostly are at the present time.

One of the best descriptions of the Visual Violet was given by Dr. M.D.S. Armour of Anstruther, Fife, in his book *Exhibition Budgerigars* , published in the 1930's. He wrote:

> . . . the body colour should be deep, even, purplish violet, quite distinct from cobalt and this intense violet should flow into the rump and tail root. The sparkle I have mentioned should be more evident in this than in any other variety; the violet should simply glow with colour. I cannot express it other than this.

European Violets

In *Budgerigar Bulletin* of March 1940 No. 52 there is an interesting reference to Violets by C. af Enehjelm, then living in Copenhagen, Denmark, giving some details of early European Violets. He writes:

> In 1929 or 1930 a well known German breeder offered Violet Budgerigars for sale in a Fancy paper. I had previously got several fine birds from this breeder and asked him for more information about this new colour. He informed me that the birds were born as really violet birds, . . . He promised to send me the best cock he had for sale. I got the bird, which really was not so much pronounced in violet but unfortunately I lost the bird before it bred.
>
> In 1934 I got a Dark Green/Blue cock from a friend. This bird was heavily suffused with blue but was bred on the colony system, so I did not know its pedigree. I paired this cock to a very nice cobalt hen, but the parents of this hen were also bred on the colony system. This pair: the dark green/blue cock and the cobalt hen had in their first nest, in addition to greens and cobalts, a chick of unusually intense colour, my first violet, a hen. In later nests the same pair gave only quite normal blue and green young.

The violet hen, paired to a cobalt cock had four or five violet young. Unfortunately I lost my violets in the Autumn, including the old hen, and only had one young violet hen left. In 1937 this young violet hen was paired to one of my best cobalt cocks and I had two nests from the pair: three violets, two cobalts and three mauves. This was the start of my violet strain . . .

These notes show clearly that Violet birds were actually being bred in Europe as far back as the late 1920's although it appeared little was known about their breeding behaviour. For a considerable time the breeding of Violets was somewhat a chancy operation, as most of those Fanciers possessing Violets did not fully understand the intricacies of their breeding behaviour. The strange thing was they did not realise that the Violet character could be possessed equally as well by Blues and Mauves as it could by Cobalts, which gave the desired visual violet colouring.

The subject of Violet breeding was much discussed by Fanciers in the Fancy Press, the *Budgerigar Bulletin* and W. Watmough in his excellent book *The Cult of the Budgerigar* gave information on matings to produce actual Visual Violets. The most extensive information was in the preliminary notes of New Colours in the *Budgerigar Matings and Colour Expectations* published in 1953 by **The Budgerigar Society**. These notes compiled by F.S. Elliott and E.W. Brooks explained in some detail just how the Dominant Violet character was actually inherited. From this point the knowledge of Violet production became much more widespread amongst Budgerigar breeders.

Garvey's Violets

Amongst the early exhibitors of the Visual Violets were Miss V.G. Scott, Mrs. W. Watmough, Mrs. M.G. Parker, Mrs. T.E. Wheeler, Harry Bryan, E.H. Stevenson, F.R. Waite, L. Trevallion and F. Garvey. It was this latter exhibitor who possessed the most brilliant and richly coloured strain of Violets in the country. Garvey's birds were well known for their beautiful pinkish tone of violet and no one else seemed to be able to produce this colour unless they had birds that came actually from the Garvey strain. It is now a considerable time since any bird of this particularly rosy violet colour have been on view at the shows as the birds seen at the present time are of a more bluish violet shade. This could mean that birds of the Garvey strain have faded out, or there may still exist remnants of the strain in some decorative aviaries where birds are not exhibited.

Varieties

All varieties of visual Violet birds are undoubtedly very handsome and exceedingly colourful, two of the most striking forms I have seen are the **Cinnamon Violet Cobalt** and the **Opaline Cinnamon Violet Cobalt.** In both instances, the addition of the Cinnamon character gives the birds a beautiful, soft, warm, rose tinted, violet shade, which is set off to perfection by their rich cinnamon markings. These two Cinnamon Violet forms are mostly desirable birds in aviaries or on the show benches, but strangely enough they are seldom seen in either places.

Another facet of the Violet character was discovered in the 1950's when birds carrying the character were crossed into Albino strains. At first these crosses came about accidentally, but when it was discovered that certain of the Albinos bred from such matings showed a rosy pink suffusion they were produced by deliberate pairings. By using Albinos that have in the first place a strong bluish suffusion, it is possible to breed **Albino Violets** with a definite pinkish suffusion on rump, flanks and underparts. Although such birds are not real pink Budgerigars they are the nearest to that colour that have so far been produced.

RED-EYED LACEWING

Since World War II only one colour mutation has occurred and been established in this country and that is the **Sex-linked Red-eyed Lacewing**. The history of these birds is rather interesting; I was told by the original Norfolk breeder, whose name I never knew, that the first Lacewing hens had appeared in his Lutino strain *after* he had introduced a Light Green cock of unknown breeding. He was most disappointed with the few badly coloured 'Lutinos' he bred in 1946/7 from this cock and a Lutino hen and quickly disposed of them, together with their green coloured nest mates.

I was intrigued by the description he had given me of these badly coloured Lutinos and tried to trace them, but without success. However, early in 1948 I did manage to trace a Green cock from the same nest as the 'bad' Lutinos and was able to buy him. He was a strong vigorous bird and I mated him with several good Normal Green and Blue hens. From these matings I obtained five Red–eyed Yellow hens with cinnamon markings and tinted tails, which for the want of a name I called Lacewings. These matings also produced numerous Green cocks and hens. From this nucleus I was able to establish this mutation in its **Green, Blue** and **Yellow-faced form.**

During the course of these cross pairings I was able to ascertain that the Lacewing character was Sex-linked and that it could be bred in all other varieties with varying depths of wing markings. In the case of the blue shades the body colour was white, but in the Yellows there were three different shades of yellow corresponding with Light, Dark and Olive Green. At one time it was suggested that Lacewings were the result of crossing Cinnamons with Lutinos (Albinos), but the many matings tried did not produce a single Lacewing. More recently the same matings have been tried again and still no Lacewings have been produced. Bearing this fact in mind it does seem that the Lacewing colouring must be due to a separate mutation.

In an article I wrote in the June 1966 *Budgerigar Bulletin* I suggested that the Budgerigar Society could now recognise the mutation and set up a **Standard**. This suggestion became a fact, as in the December 1968 *Budgerigar Bulletin* a **Standard** and a **Scale of Points** for the Lacewings were published, and so the fifth member of the sex-linked colours became established.

Exhibiting

I exhibited the first **Lacewing Yellow** hen at the National in 1951 and she was not placed in the cards, although she was much discussed amongst breeders. However, in 1956, a young **Lacewing White** cock I bred won in an Any Other Colour class of thirty three entries, which I think was the first win for a Lacewing cock. For some years small numbers of Lacewings were regularly exhibited at shows up and down the country and then their popularity began to fade. In the late 1970's a few rather nice examples of Lacewing hens appeared in some exhibition strains and this caused a number of breeders to take a renewed interest in this mutation. At the 1979 National Exhibition, indeed, Miss J.E. Dempster of Axminster, Devon, late of Australia, showed some six examples of the Lacewing Yellow and this was the first time for quite some years that more than the odd example had been on view. Miss Dempster had a good stud of Lacewings whilst in Australia but she had to leave them all behind, because of the export ban, when she came to live in Great Britain. Her new stock are a combination of British and South African birds and were of fine exhibition type with plenty of substance and style and should certainly help to further increase their breeding amongst Fanciers.

Being a Sex-linked colour there are always more hens bred than cock birds in this Lacewing strain, and these hens mostly stem from normally coloured cocks that are split for Lacewing often unbeknown to the breeder. It now seems that Lacewings are likely to make a comeback as an exhibition variety and will certainly add further interest to the Any Other Colour Sections at shows.

Overseas Interest

During the period when Lacewings were being bred more freely, overseas fanciers became interested and I sent examples to America, Australia, South Africa and Europe. Until I lost contact with those breeders I heard that Lacewings were being produced from the original stock to the third and fourth generations. It is to be hoped that some birds from these strains are still being bred in these countries.

FEATHER MUTATIONS — CRESTED BUDGERIGARS

Before giving details of other colour mutations, that have appeared and then either have been lost or not officially recognised, I must discuss an important feather mutation — the Crest.

Origin

The first news that Crested Budgerigars were in existence and being bred in Great Britain came from a note from Mrs. Brown of Morcombe, Lancs, that appeared in The *Budgerigar Bulletin* of December 1938 No. 48, from which I quote the following extract:

> Now that I have introduced to Budgerigar breeders in this country the Crested type, I think it will be of interest to say that this variety was purely accidental. Mr. Matthews of Kogarah, New South Wales, noticed one of a brood of Yellow/Whites, from the parents of just ordinary importance, had the feathers on the head curled towards the front and sides, giving the appearance of a crest in making. By the time this bird reached maturity the crest has improved to such an extent that Mr. Matthews realised he possessed a Budgerigar of outstanding importance . . . This bird, when matured was paired to its mother; from this mating there were crests, half crests and split crests. Mr. Matthews has now in his aviary crests of the third and fourth generation. The accompanying illustration is of a bird of the third generation.

This illustration shows what we know today as a **Full Circular Crest**. I think that the Half Crests Mrs. Brown mentioned must be either Half Circular or Tufted.

This would indicate that the Australian Crested mutation must have occurred somewhere about 1933 as Mrs. Brown was breeding birds of that strain in 1938. However two other Crested mutations were known to exist after the Australian one, the first being in North America and the second of European origin. The fourth edition of the *Handbook of The Crested Budgerigar Club* published in 1980 gives the following information on the first Crests:

> . . . There is little doubt that the first crested budgerigar appeared in Sydney, Australia, about 1920, this being the earliest record we have of them. As there was no control over their export by the Australian authorities at that time, it is, of course, possible that some may have found their way to other lands but no evidence of this has yet been found.
>
> On the other hand, crests appeared on the Continent just prior to the second

Figure 6.2 Types of Crest — Full Circular Crest
courtesy: **Crested Budgerigar Club**

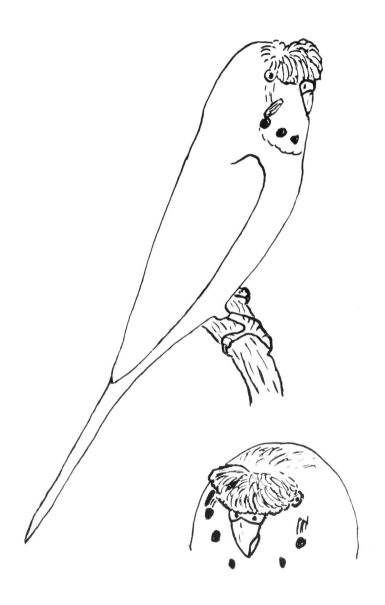

Figure 6.3   Half Circular Crest
courtesy: **Crested Budgerigar Club**

Figure 6.4   Tufted Crest
courtesy: **Crested Budgerigar Club**

world war and has the opportunity to go anywhere for that short period and there is evidence that we have their descendants with us to this day. This is one of the two major sources of crested Budgerigars we have here in Britain.

The other source of which we have any information is that a crest mutant occurred in Canada round about 1948 in the aviary of Mrs. W.B. Knights of Nova Scotia, although there is a conflicting report that they first appeared before that in another establishment in Toronto. Still, it appears distinctly Canadian in origin and they have sufficient slight peculiarities to identify them from the Continental variety . . .

It will be noted that there is a difference in the dates of the appearance of the Australian mutation; the record just mentioned states about 1920 but Mrs. Brown's information is some dozen years later in a different part of the country. Of course the later 'mutation' could have been derived from the earlier one, or they may have been quite separate occurrences. It is known that Crested birds from both America and Europe were imported into Great Britain, I myself had Full Circular Crests from Holland in 1948 and I know other breeders received birds from the same source and also some American stock. This means that present day British Crested Budgerigars could have their origin in all three of these known and recorded Crest mutations.

Exhibition

It will have been noticed that although Crested Budgerigars actually came into existence some forty five years ago it is only comparatively in recent times that they have come into prominence as exhibition birds. For a great many years Crests were mainly bred in the aviaries of non exhibiting fanciers who bred for colour, and conseqently the majority of Crested birds available were of the rare or more unusual colours and did not attract the big exhibiting breeders. Nevertheless, in 1962 the small number of Crest breeding enthusiasts, on the initiative of Alan F. Fullilove, then of Feltham, Middlesex, felt the breed should be organised and suggested that a **Specialist Club** for the promotion of Crests should be inaugurated.

The Club was founded in May 1962 under the auspices of myself as President with A.F. Fullilove Secretary, J.H. Pincombe Treasurer and K.P. Pugh in the Chair, and a little later C.N. Kerry took the position of Show Patronage Secretary, together with a committee of four. In due course it was agreed that *Standards* should be evolved for the three distinct kinds of Crests — the **Full Circular,** the **Half Circular** and the **Tufted**, with an accompanying **scale of points**. This was done in conjunction with drawings showing the ideal for each kind of Crest using the **Budgerigar Society's Ideal Bird** (1966) as a basis.

Up to the formation of the Crested Budgerigar Club the few Crests that were shown appeared in the A.O.C. classes. When separate classes

CRESTED BUDGERIGAR CLUB

Standard for Crested Budgerigars

CRESTED LIGHT GREEN

Head: Ornamented with a Circular type, a Half–Circular type or a Tufted type of crest.

Mask: Buttercup of an even tone ornamented on each side with three clearly defined round black spots, one of which appears at the base of each cheek patch.

Cheek Patches: Violet.

General body colour: Back, rump, breast, flanks and underparts bright grass green of a solid and even shade throughout; markings on cheeks, back of head, neck and wings black and well defined on a Buttercup ground.

Tail: Two long feathers blue–black.

Circular Crest: This should be a flat round crest with the feathers radiating from the centre of the head.

Tail: Two long feathers blue–black.

Half Circular Crest: This should be a half circle of feathers falling or raised in a fringe above the cere.

Tufted Crest: This should be an upright crest of feathers up to three–eighths of an inch high rising just above the cere.

The above is the standard for the Light Green Crested form, all other colours will be on similar lines with the change of colour where appropriate.

Scale of points:

Size, shape, balance deportment & condition	Size & shape of crest	Colour & Wing Markings	Mask & Spots
35	40	15	10

With varieties not having throat spots and wing markings, the points will be allocated to colour.

General Notes

Type. These standards should be used in conjunction with the C.B.C. Pictorial Ideal for three distinct types of crest.

Condition. The birds must be in good health with no broken or missing feathers or spiky quills within its crest. It must stand steady on the perch, looking alert and fearless with the eyes bold and bright.

Shape of Crest. The shape of each type of crest should be well–defined and any untidy feather disturbance(s) a fault.

Size. Eight and a half inches from crown of the head to the tip of the tail without any "long-flighted" characteristics.

N.B. Crested Budgerigars must be shown in B.S. approved showcages.

Figure 6.5 Crested Budgerigar Club Standard for Crested Budgerigars

were provided by The Crested Budgerigar Club Patronage many more Crested birds were benched. I think it can be said that the real turning point for the Crested varieties came when the Club became an Associate Member of **The Budgerigar Society**. Some excellent black and white photographs of the three kinds of Crests together with the Crested Budgerigar Club's line drawings appeared in the September 1968 Issue of the *Budgerigar Bulletin*. Classes for Crests were then scheduled at The Club Show, Bingley Halls, Leicester, and the National Exhibition of Cage and Aviary Birds, Alexander Palace, London.

Early Exhibitors

Amongst the early exhibitors from the Crested Budgerigar Club were Squadron Leader S.A. Luxford, M.B.E., A.F. Fullilove, C.F. Kerry, A.M. Cooper, J.W. Phillips and K.P. Pugh with most of the birds exhibited being of the Full Crested type. At the Budgerigar Society's Club Show in 1978 there were some eighty Crests from twenty-two exhibitors split about equally between adult and breeders birds. Crests have now become a regular Section at many shows and are always an attraction to both fanciers and visitors.

Inheritance Theories

For some long time before the Crested Budgerigar Club was founded, breeders of Crested Budgerigars were puzzled by the inheritance of this feather character and various theories were expounded. None of these fitted all the different breeding results but the **Inhibitor Theory** seems to have had the best possibilities. This theory is well explained in *The Crested Budgerigar Society's Handbook* edited by A.F. Fullilove from which I give the following notes: The germ of the inhibitor principle first appeared to the present writer in the Autumn of 1962 when studying the problem of why there should be three types of Crest in Budgerigars, whereas all other species have only one, and why non–crested progeny appeared even from Crest x Crest matings. The supposition that all non-crests from Crest x Crest matings are genetically Crested was considered, but the presence of an inhibiting influence completely suppresses any appearance of a crest in these birds. The same restricting agent would be at work in the Tufted birds showing it to be weakening slightly with the Half Crest being at half strength and completely absent in the Full Crest.

In the August 1963 Issue of The Budgerigar Society of Australasia magazine, *The Budgerigar*, D. Burke of Sydney outlined a similar idea, except that it was in reverse; he believed the crest needed an additional influence to allow it to appear, but sufficient information was not given to form a basis of a proper theory of inheritance. The Editor's own theory was published in the *C.B.C. Newsletter* at about the same time, but this also did not give the complete picture.

The discussions with Cyril Warner made it clear that it did not wholly fit the facts and that a better formula to describe the action of the inhibiting force was required. The present inhibitor theory was then proposed and accepted by Cyril Warner as a considerable improvement, with some evidence to support what he had found.

In the meantime, Dr. J. Eugene Fox, Head of the Department of Botany, Kansas University, U.S.A. had studied the Newsletter article in the light of the 1963 Crest breeding results and presented his own version of the Inhibitor Theory which was published in *Cage and Aviary Birds* in the 28th of May, 1964, Issue. It was practically identical with the theory as agreed with Cyril Warner, except the genetical symbols were different. To avoid confusion it was decided that Dr. Fox's genetical formula would be used to explain the Inhibitor Theory.

The basis of the theory is that the genetic factor for Crests is dominant to non-Crests but its expression is influenced by at least one pair of modifying genes. Thus the Crested character depends upon the balance between two genes for crest determination and two genes for crest repression situated on their respective chromosomes.

From this it will be seen that the passing on of the Crested character is somewhat more complex than the ordinary colour characters, although it follows the usual Mendelian Principles of Inheritance and makes their production exceedingly interesting. I have not gone too deeply into the production of the various Crested birds as this is a subject to be dealt with under genetical inheritance of the Budgerigar, and is quite distinct from their history.

LONG FLIGHTED MUTATION

The crest is not the only feather mutation that has occurred amongst Budgerigars, as some time after the Second World War a strange and important feather mutation, in some respects, occurred, but the place and time where it occurred has never been defined as far as I have been able to trace. This mutation, generally known as Long-flighted, caused the feathers to grow to a far greater length than normal, giving such birds a strange elongated appearance.

Exhibiting

Such birds had large heads, flat narrow chests, long drooping flight feathers and exceedingly long tails. Because of their size, Long-flighted birds were shown and some actually won prizes at these shows. It soon became evident that Long-flighted birds were abnormal and did not meet the Budgerigar Society's *Standard* and in its wisdom the Budgerigar Society barred these from taking any awards. This directive met with the approval of the vast majority of exhibitors and Long-flighted specimens disappeared from the show benches.

Breeding and the Ideal Standard

Although the Long-flighted birds had gone from the shows their presence in the breeding quarters persisted for some time. Breeders had found that certain of the characteristics possessed by the Long-flighted could be introduced to improve the ordinary stock. The larger size and shape of head, depth of mask, and longer feathers, are some of the factors now incorporated in the modern exhibition Budgerigars. If the pre-war *Ideal Standards* are compared with those of the 1960's it will be seen what changes came to the Exhibition birds of that period. A further change in the *Ideal Standard* came again in the 1970's and there have been even further alterations made in the 1980's. Changes in shape may look all right on paper, but when it comes to the living creatures it is often quite another matter. From what I have seen of some of the suggestions, the birds would be far too top heavy to be able to hold themselves on their perches at the required angle for show birds. There is always need for caution when attempting to bring about structural changes, as Nature will only permit breeders to go so far before bringing in a lethal veto.

FEATHER DUSTERS

Evidence of Nature's limiting veto will be found in another feather mutation that has occurred amongst exhibition stock in recent years, and that is the so-called Feather Dusters. These birds are large with big heads and very long feathers growing out at all angles from the body. Needless to say, they cannot fly and spend what little time they have scrambling about on the floor of the cage or aviary. As far as I have been able to discover the longest time one of these monstrosities has lived or shall we say existed is seventeen months, generally they die within a matter of weeks or months. The parents of Feather Dusters always seem to be fine looking healthy show type birds and none have been bred from the ordinary, aviary type Budgerigars.

Early Breeding

Two Feather Dusters bred by Tom North together with their parents, a pair of Whitewings, were on display at The Budgerigar Society's Convention held in Harrogate, Yorkshire, in 1975, in the Unusual and Rare Colour Section. This was, I think, the first time two such birds had been on public display in Great Britain. The March 1961 Issue of *The Budgerigar Bulletin* contains an article, together with a photograph of a Feather Duster that was bred in Australia by G. Young of Strathmore, Melbourne, Australia. The writer of the article, E. Wilson of Victoria, Australia, said these were bred in the second nest from a pair of Greens, one a Blue died and the other two, Greens, lived and were shown to the public. Mr. Young bred several more of these Feather Dusters last year (1960) from the same pair of Greens. It was also reported that Feather Dusters were bred in a number of other aviaries in different parts of Australia.

Reports from various parts of the country indicate that the number of Feather Dusters bred each season has been steadily on the increase since the first examples appeared. This would seem to indicate that the gene for this abnormality is being transmitted from strain to strain. There is no way in which carriers of the Recessive Feather Duster gene can be visually detected, the breeder's first knowledge is their sudden appearance in the nest. It is quite clear that this mutation is not going to help in the development of Budgerigars in any way and every effort should be made to eradicate it from strains. If the parents, brothers and sisters, of Feather Dusters are not used for further breeding purposes it will go a long way to stop the progression of this undesirable character.

Figure 6.6   Feather Duster

FEATHERED LEGS AND FEET

Over the years a few birds have been bred with some feathers on their feet and legs, and fortunately, because these feathers looked unsightly and made closed ringing difficult, no attempts to develop such birds have been made.

I had an example of such a bird in the 1950's, a Light Green hen, with six feathers on one leg and five on the other; she was bred from two quite unrelated, normal-looking light green birds. Paired to an unrelated Light Green cock, the pair produced four youngsters, one having feathers on its legs like the mother. This showed the character to be a Dominant and therefore easily eradicable from a strain, this I promptly did. A few other fanciers who have also had the odd bird with feathers on their legs have told me they too found the character Dominant but did not persist with their breeding.

AVIARY HOUSING

One unusual, and interesting, aspect of budgerigar keeping was given by his Grace, the 8th Duke of Bedford, who kept and bred Homing Budgerigars in an aviary at his home, Woburn Abbey, Bedfordshire. Whilst establishing his flock of Homing birds the late Duke wrote a most instructive book based on his own satisfactory achievements with Budgerigars at liberty. The introduction to his little book sums up the enterprise exceeding well:

> Since the first advent of Homing flocks of Budgerigars were pioneered by the Duke this method of keeping them has found favour in various parts of the country where the conditions are suitable. One notable free flying flock is owned by Her Majesty Queen Elizabeth II and are housed in the grounds of Windsor Castle.
>
> It will I know be realised that the aviary door cannot just be opened and the birds will fly in and out at will. It takes some preparation both of the aviary and the birds to start a flock of free flying Budgerigars. Firstly, the aviary itself has to be sited correctly and in the right surroundings. The exits and inlets of the aviary have to be of a special design and the birds have to be trained to use them. This training can be given to Budgerigars bred under any conditions providing it is carried out at certain times of their lives. Under these free flying conditions there are bound to be some losses in the flock through natural causes, predators and birds straying away from their own area. Such losses are more than balanced by the young produced and numbers have to be reduced periodically and sometimes fresh stock introduced to prevent inbreeding. Once a flock has been established it will provide the owner with endless pleasure with very little trouble.

Figure 6.7 Larger garden aviaries — views of Aviaries near Sydney, Australia in the 1930's.

CHAPTER 7

UNSUCCESSFUL MUTATIONS; CURRENT AND FUTURE DEVELOPMENTS

Undoubtedly colour mutations have occurred in mixed breeding collections of Budgerigars that have not been recorded and, possibly, not noticed by their breeders; thus they have vanished, but may reappear at some other time. In other cases, mutations have been recorded and developed for a time and then through various reasons have disappeared from the scene.

SELF BLUE

One example of a mutation which failed to establish itself, is recorded in the *Budgerigar Bulletin* No. 41 of March 1937 in an article by E. Cooper of St. Albans, Hertfordshire, headed **The Self Blue Budgerigar**. I quote from this article:

In 1934 I had a Greywing Blue/White cock which had a fair amount of bloom on the back of its head, neck and shoulders. Breeders are familiar with this bloom which is often seen in an adult bird that is in good condition. In this bird the bloom consisted of a light, though well defined bluish tinge, extending from the skull to the middle of the back. There was also a distinct blue colouration between the wing striations. This bird, when mated to a white cobalt hen, produced nine youngsters and these birds when adult showed little intensification of the bloom. A daughter having the greatest amount of bloom was paired back to its father. This mating also produced nine youngsters. The flesh of the newly hatched chicks was very pale compared with that of normal nestlings. They appeared to be anaemic and almost bloodless. Four died before feathering was completed and nothing unusual was noticed in the colour of the nest feathers of the remaining birds. One bird when four months old and completed its moult had new feathers that were self blue on head, neck, shoulders and wings, but died soon after. Another bird, a greywing blue cock, had its adult colour described as opaline but Opalines had not then been bred in this country. The blue continued right down the back and the grey wing markings were imposed on a ground colour of blue, instead of white as in the normal bird . . . In 1936 results were extremely disappointing. A large number of chicks were hatched, but many died in the nest and of the survivors a large proportion died during the first moult and

117

all the latter birds were beginning to assume the blue plumage. I am perfectly certain that these birds are not Opalines and I believe they constitute an entirely new mutation. As far as I can ascertain the factors concerned are controlled by sex. By this I do not mean that inheritance is necessarily sex-linked as for example in the well known case of the Cinnamon. Results tend to prove that the inheritance follows the simple Mendelian Laws and that this mutation is affected by secondary sexual characters . . . It is impossible to distinguish these blue birds from the non blue birds until adult plumage is assumed. All the blue birds are cocks though all the hens show a slight amount of bloom . . . In the case of these blue birds it has been noted that the blue plumage is not assumed until maturity has been reached and then the cocks assume a beautiful and brilliant blue sheen from head to tail. In the light of present knowledge, one can only conclude that this mutation depends to a large extent on sex hormones.

The question of this self Blue mutation was discussed by Mr. Cooper with numerous fanciers who were interested in breeding new varieties at that particular period, and their observations were forwarded to Professor Crew for his expert opinion. Mr. Cooper sent his breeding records together with some live examples of these birds to Professor Crew, who replied in the following note:

The self blue is of particular interest in that, from Mr. Cooper's results, the suggestion emerges that the character self colour behaves as a dominant with an intermediate expression in the heterozygous condition. The fact that the full expression of this character seems to be restricted to males also strongly suggests that the action of this gene is influenced very largely by the male sex hormone. This being so, it would follow naturally that the character would appear fully only in males. This would constitute an excellent example of a sex limited character. It is important to distinguish between a sex limited and a sex-linked character. The character is sex-linked solely for the reason that its gene is carried on the X chromosome. A sex limited character, on the other hand, is exhibited in the plumage only by one sex. Though both sexes can carry the gene, its expression is determined by the physiological environment in which it finds itself . . . Before a great deal of fascinating experimental work is carried out information must be sought to discover the reason for its apparent lethal effect upon the males that carry the character . . .

It will be seen from these extracts and Professor Crew's comments that this mutation operates in quite a different manner to all the others that have been produced so far. Although Mr. Cooper tried very hard to develop the strain he was not able to maintain it for more than a few years before it finally petered out. I saw some of these self blue birds at Mr. Cooper's aviaries and their colouring was certainly quite different and distinct from any of the Opaline forms which came into being soon after that time.

Exhibiting

A few examples of these self blue birds did find their way on to the show bench. At the Bird Fancy National Exhibition held in the New Horticultural Hall, London, in December 1936 E. Cooper exhibited one of his Self Blues for the first time. At this period Opalines were only just making their debut in this country and certainly Mr. Cooper had none in his possession. In the A.O.C. class at the following year's Bird Fancy Exhibition E. Cooper exhibited three specimens of the Self Blues, one of which was placed Third out of a total of twenty-three entries. As far as I have been able to trace, this was the last time Self Blues of this mutation were seen on the show bench and in fact by the Fancy in general. From time to time birds have been bred that have possessed an extra amount of bloom on their plumage but they have all reproduced in the ordinary manner and have not approached the Cooper Self Blues for richness of colour. Such birds have been called **Intensives** and **Iridescents** but up to the present do not seem to have been established as definite varieties.

GREYWING YELLOWS AND OTHER WING-MARKED YELLOWS

Soon after the Australian Clearwings had been recognised as a distinct and definite mutation reports began to come to hand that new kinds of yellow birds were being produced. From Australia came the news that birds known as Greywing Yellows were being bred, although this idea was at first dismissed by breeders in this country as being impossible. Nevertheless, I received skins of these birds from Australia and they were certainly yellow birds with grey wing markings, distinct throat spots and light bluish grey tails.

In the March 1939 *Budgerigar Bulletin* No. 49 Miss Kirkby-Mason gave information that she had, in 1938, bred birds from a pair of exhibition Yellows that were similar to the Australian type, one specimen being shown as a Greywing Yellow at the Caterham Show. After a time no further news was heard about the establishment as a breeding strain of these birds so it can be concluded that they must have faded out. It would appear, however, that the Australian mutation persisted, as I have had letters in 1975 and 1979 from breeders in Sydney, Australia, and another from one in New Zealand that they were still breeding Greywing Yellows. This, together with other reports, make it clear that the existence of such birds must be taken as a fact, as the mutation has persisted for so many years and they are quite distinct from Yellows of deep suffusion that can also have quite dark markings.

Yellow with Dark Undulations

A further form of wing marked Yellow came into the possession of Scott and Campkin of Cambridge about 1933/34, and was reported in the *Budgerigar Bulletin* of June 1934. This Yellow was described as having black wings and tail without any undulating markings on its back; the

119

black colouring starting about halfway down the length of the wings. Although the colour appeared to be black, each feather was actually very dark green on one side and black on the other. It was hoped that this coloration would prove to be inheritable and not due to some temporary disarrangement of the colouring agents.

In the following *Bulletin* came the news that this cock bird, paired to a normal Light Yellow hen had produced only green coloured young ones. This would be in line if the colouring was a Recessive one or due to a temporary fault in the colouring agents. Unfortunately it was proved by breeding to be the latter and no further examples were bred through this bird. Further examples of Yellow with dark undulations have been reported from Germany, France, Belgium and Holland, all of which appeared to be due to causes that could not be inherited.

Australian Blackwings

In 1979 I had reports of further **Greywing Yellows** and **Greywing Whites** being bred in Australia by R. Hancock of Beverley, South Australia, who also had a strain of Blackwing (normal wing) Yellows and Whites breeding in his aviaries for many years. Although Mr. Hancock had been breeding Blackwings since the middle of the 1930's, so they are well established, their existence does not appear to have been previously recorded, as far as I can trace, in Budgerigar literature in this country. It would seem that Greywing Yellows and Greywing Whites, or Silvers as they are often called in Australia, are a firmly established type in that country. Although the strains are breeding in widely separated areas it is quite possible they were all derived from a common source.

I have seen a wing from one of the Greywing Yellow kind and it was marked similarly to that found sometimes on heavily wing marked Yellow-wing Greens. There is however a distinct difference between the two; whereas the underside of the wing butts of Yellow-wings are green, to match their body colour, those of the Greywing Yellows are definitely yellow, in keeping with their body colour. From what I hear, the American Greywing Yellows are of similar colouring and may well have been derived in the first case from the Australian mutation. I do not know how these Greywing Yellows and Greywing Whites fit into the genetical pattern, they may of course come in with the Greywing, Clearwing, Dilute (Yellow and White) multiple Allelomorph, although they could be on quite a distinct chromosome. If birds were available in Great Britain they would make a very interesting course of experimental crossings. I have recently heard that Dr. H. Harrison of Co. Wicklow, Eire, also has a small flock of Greywing Yellows derived from a mutant which appeared in a breeder friend's aviary.

American (Papin) Clear-Bodies

The Australian Blackwing variety, mentioned in a previous paragraph, shows a great similarity to the American strain of birds, known there as Clear-bodies. These **American Clear-bodies** came to notice during the middle 1950's and it would seem all at about the same period in three separate locations. In his excellent book (now out of print) *Exhibition Budgerigars*, Dr. M.D.S. Armour gives a coloured plate of an Opaline form of a Black-wing Yellow. It is described in the manuscript as a Laced Yellow, a possible bird of the future. In actual fact the Australian Black-wing mutation was being bred before the book was published, although the author had no knowledge at that time that such birds existed.

I saw some coloured sketches and feathers from the American Clear-bodies when they were first being evolved and they showed the birds as having black or near black markings with a more or less clear body colour of yellow. It may well be that all the Clear-bodied owe their colouring to a single mutation which has appeared in quite a number of different places in the world. To support this assumption from information to hand through Australian breeders it would seem that the Greywing Yellows of Mr. Hancock were derived from his original Blackwing strain. This being so, it could follow that the American Clear-bodies have produced the American Greywing Yellows. Bearing these points in mind it would be logical to think that there can be a Clear-body kind of most of the other varieties.

Until enough breeding stock becomes available for controlled experimental work and the precise nature of the inheritance and the relationship of the different strains of wing marked Clear-bodied kinds are firmly established, we can only speculate. This extract from a letter I had from Gay Terrance and Kathleen Papin of California, U.S.A. dated 10th November 1958 gives the history of the Papin Clear-bodies:

We have produced a full nest of Clear-bodies, two of which have clear yellow rumps, though they kept the green saddle and green in the wings. We have had to retain and breed many birds, trying to develop a strain which will produce 100% Clear-bodies. The original hen was a pure Opaline Green and the cock was a Green/Opaline Blue so it was several generations before we had any Blues and only this year we produced a Blue which also carried the Clear-body factor. We believe these are one factor birds as they still have quite a bit of blue on them.

We are of the opinion that a one factor Clear-body shows a certain degree of depigmentation and that the bird with the yellow (or white) body is the two factor bird. Our nest of Clear-bodies were produced from the two factor birds . . .

Our best Clear-bodies come from the Light Green Opaline matings but if the body colour could be cleared sufficiently on the Olive Green Opaline, the yellow would be much richer.

The original Clear-body Opaline hens were quite green as babies but by their

second or third moult they were very clear on the breast with much yellow on the rump. I shouldn't have said quite green as they were more yellow than green but there was green showing . . . There are many matings to produce Clear-bodies but the one I give is the one we use to produce the latest nest of all clear bodies. Because the original hen was such a poor specimen and the cock was such a handsome and friendly fellow, we are inclined to give him more than his share of credit. The line we intended to establish from the outcross showed nothing of value unless paired back to the original mutants. The hen was able to produce birds with depigmentation no matter what her mate was. We gained in the long run as we probably would have lost out on type completely had we relied on her.

. . . Why do you think Clear-body appeared in Opaline and what is keeping us from getting Clear-body Normals? I don't know of any other variety which appears in one without showing it in the other also.

It will be of great interest when examples of Clear–bodies come to Great Britain so that we can carry out experimental crosses with other varieties. I have in mind one special cross that of Clear-body to Clearwing. Will such a cross give Normal birds or something quite new?

THE FADED COLOURS

Some time in late 1932 N.A. Coulson of Lincoln had a mutation appear amongst his stock of Normals which had an eye colour between that of the English Fallow and the Cinnamon. For the want of a better name he called his birds **Faded Greens, Faded Blues** and so on. The original bird, a cock, looked just like a dull example of a Greywing Green except that its eyes were a solid plum shade. At that time Mr. Coulson did not think much about this bird, but when he paired it to an ordinary Greywing Green/Blue hen the pair gave only normally coloured Green and Blue chicks. This breeding result indicated, of course, that it was not a Normal Greywing but another similarly coloured mutation. The cock bird was next mated with a White Blue and again only normally coloured Greens and Blues were produced. In 1935 the original Faded Green cock was mated with one of his daughters and others of his progeny were mated *inter se*. From these crosses came further examples of Faded Greens and Faded Blues together with some Faded Yellows, White and Greywings. All these colours were dull and only about half the intensity of their Normal counterparts.

These results prove clearly that the Faded colour phase was a definite Recessive mutation and one that could be bred in examples of all other established varieties. When the Faded character was combined with another colour character the resulting birds were half the normal colouring and all had plum coloured eyes. I would say that Cinnamon and the Red-eyed kinds were not used in any experimental pairings with Faded birds. For the first few days after hatching the colour of the eyes of all the Faded birds was like that of the German Fallow but slowly changing to the plum shade as the birds developed.

Exhibiting

Through the kindness of Mr. Coulson I was able to add Faded birds to my stud and carried out many cross pairings with them, ultimately getting numerous Faded birds in most colours. A few other breeders of that time beside Mr. Coulson and myself had these Faded birds and some examples were actually exhibited. Owing to their similarity in colour to the Greywings, which were then exceedingly popular, they did not attract many breeders. With the outbreak of War in 1939 and the resulting drastic reduction in stocks of Budgerigars in Great Britain, the breeding of Faded Greens ceased and this Recessive mutation disappeared; for good I thought.

Reappearance

In the early 1970's, however, whilst looking over a breeding collection of mixed colours in the little Suffolk town of Leiston, I thought I saw a nicely coloured Greywing Dark Green cock. The owner said I could have the bird if I liked to catch him — this I promptly did. The parentage of this bird could not be traced as there were some dozen or so breeding pairs of mixed colours in the colony. When I got the bird home I examined him closely and it was then I saw that his eyes were plum coloured just like the old Faded Greens.

In due course I paired him, first with a Light Yellow to see if his breeding behaviour was the same as that of the Faded birds. From the Yellow/White hen I had four young normally coloured Light Green cocks so I paired him next to a Sky Blue, again four chicks, three Green cocks and one Green hen. I now had the original Faded cock, seven split cocks and only one split hen, which I paired back to her sire the following season. This mating gave two Faded Green hens, one Faded Blue hen, one Faded Dark Green cock, together with a number of normally coloured cocks. The following year I put the Faded Green to a half brother of the previous season's breeding with the high hopes of getting further Faded cocks and hens. Unfortunately, this Faded Green hen proved to be a non-breeder so after two clutches of two eggs each she completely lost all interest in further breeding activities.

The other Faded Green hen and the Faded Blue hen both died without producing any offspring and the Faded Dark Green cock showed no interest at all in the opposite sex. This left me with the original cock and quite a number of split cocks several of which I mated to pure Normals but only got a few further cock birds. After struggling to revive the Faded character for several years it slipped once again into oblivion. It is quite possible that the Faded mutation has appeared in

123

other colony breeding flocks and being similar to the Greywing in colour has escaped notice and therefore failed to become established. Some keen and watchful breeder may spot the mutation again in the future and it will in time be added to our long list of established mutations.

BROWNWINGS

From reading published literature, it has not been possible to find out just when or where the mutation called Brownwing began its existence. It may, possibly, have occurred during or just after the last war period and came to notice in the late 1940's or early 1950's. In the Seventh Edition of the book of *Budgerigar Matings and Colour Expectations*, Brownwings are briefly described and breeding rules for both **Green** and **Blue series** given. In their book, *Genetics for Budgerigar Breeders** Taylor & Warner mention the Brownwings as being a Recessive variety but no information on their origin is given.

A few examples I saw were very similar in their colouring to the well known Cinnamons, but of a duller tone throughout. They lacked too the pink eye colour which is the characteristic of all Cinnamon varieties when first hatched, having at all times the usual dark eyes of Normals. From correspondence I had with breeders it would seem that most Brownwings were bred in Lancashire and a few examples were exhibited in that area. Because of their similarity in colour to the bright Sex-linked Cinnamons, which were easy to breed, the Brownwings did not become popular and eventually the strains faded out.

At the end of 1939 I had a letter dated December 5th from L. Raymaekers of Brussels, Belgium, a well known bird breeder giving me some particulars and enclosing a wing from a variety he called Brownwing, and said it was Recessive in its breeding behaviour. From this information and examination of the wing I came to the conclusion that these birds had been developed from Clearwings. It was known at that time that certain Clearwings carried quite heavy, wide markings on their wings and if bred through Opalines these markings assumed a definite bronze brown shade. I think that the Raymaeker Brownwings were selectively bred from such birds and showed an excess of brown colouring in their wing markings combined with a deep body shade both in the Blue and Green kinds. As far as I have been able to trace this particular strain of birds did not survive over the war years, and I have not heard of them since. The British race of Brownwings were undoubtedly a definite mutation and quite different in their overall

*Published by Illiffe Books, 1961.

colouring to the Continental kind which were probably a selectively bred colour phase.

SPANGLES

Early in 1978 news was brought to this country by A. Vousden of Old Coulsden, Surrey, who, whilst visiting his daughter in Australia, had seen some Budgerigars with colouring quite new to him. Because of their attractive pattern markings these have been called Spangles by their breeders. Mr. Vousden saw and examined these new birds in three different breeding establishments where they were produced in Green, Blue, Opaline and Yellow forms. More particulars of these Spangles are given in the Budgerigar Society of Australia's magazine *Budgie Digest* of March/April 1978 by Frank Gardener of Melbourne who is one of the breeders of these birds.

It would appear that this mutation may first have occurred in a breeding colony of mixed colours, but it is difficult to obtain precise details. Several breeders in various parts of the country had these birds at about the same time, so they may all have had a common source or, of course, there could have been several spontaneous mutations. In the course of his Article Mr. Gardener gives *Colour Standards* for several colours of these Spangles one of which I will give as a sample:

Spangle Cobalt: Mask white, throat spots black with white centre, cheek patches violet, body colour cobalt, wing markings with each feather edged with black, flight feathers white edged with black, tail white edged with black.

Inheritance Characteristics

Spangles follow an unusual manner of inheritance, one that is not frequently met with in the now known mutations of Budgerigars. The character that causes this delightful spangled pattern is a Dominant one and like other Dominant characters can be had in a single or double quantity. A single character Spangle, cock or hen, paired to any normal colour will give half Spangles and half Normals as is usual in a Dominant inheritance. When two single character Spangles are paired together they again give the normal Mendelian percentages of 25% Normal, 50% Single character Spangles and 25% double character Spangles. However the spangled pattern effect on the double character birds is quite faint giving practically a clear wing but when paired to Normals they give all ordinary marked Spangles. As the Spangle can be had in all other varieties and colours it will be possible to breed some most exciting coloured birds in the future.

125

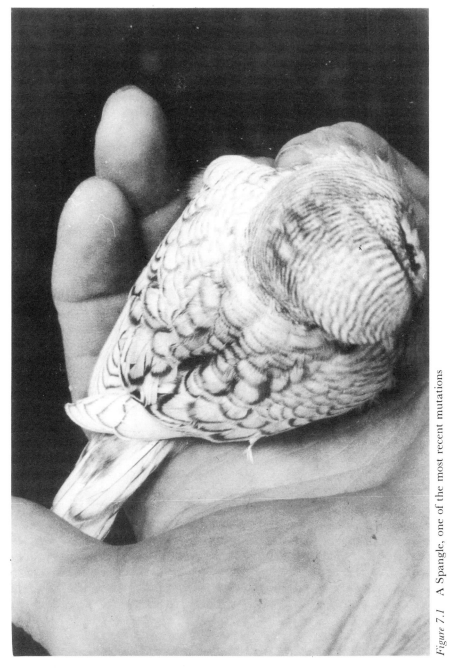

Figure 7.1 A Spangle, one of the most recent mutations

126

AUSTRALIAN PIED

Before the Spangle mutations appeared in Australia I had news of a further kind of Pied being bred by a lady Fancier in that country. These birds are quite unlike all other known Pied Budgerigars as they have quite normally coloured plumage in their nest feather, it is only when they assume their first adult feathers that pied areas start to develop. I gathered from my discussions with Dr. Harold Cooper that this Pied form is still being bred by a few Fanciers in Australia, although the original breeder has died. A strange thing about this Pied form is that the Pied areas actually increase with each successive moult with the main pied areas being on the lower part of the body. This is the first time that this particular form of pied markings has been found in Budgerigars but I have been told it does occur periodically with some other Parrot-like species.

COMPOSITE FORMS

I have now discussed in some detail the origins of the various mutations that have been noted amongst Budgerigars in different parts of the world and these are not the final total. In the following period of time there will, no doubt, be other mutations appearing although not as frequently as previously experienced. There are of course a tremendous number of possible combinations of the existing characters, large numbers of which have already been produced by enterprising breeders adding variety to both aviary and show bench. I do not intend to quote all these exciting composite birds but would like to mention two which have been bred, although not for some considerable time.

Synthetic Albino

By combining certain existing colour characters of a bird, it is possible to breed a synthetic form of another. The first examples of this are the **Cinnamon Fallow Whites** and **Cinnamon Fallow Yellows,** a combination which gives birds that look like Albinos and Lutinos. It was in an article by myself, published in *The Bird Fancy* Issue of November 7th 1936, and a further one in February 20th 1937 that the first breeding of such a combination was given. This synthetic Albino, a hen, was produced in the aviaries of J.W. Pretty of Cambridge, who was one of the first breeders of the German Fallow variety. This hen came from a Normal Cobalt/Cinnamon Fallow White cock and a Fallow Cobalt/White hen and was the last chick in a nest of five. When seen beside the usual sex-linked Albinos these composite birds are exactly the same colourwise. In a most explanatory article in *The Budgerigar Bulletin*

127

No. 41 of March 1937 F.G. North of Esher, Surrey, gave details of pairings which would produce these synthetic Albinos and Lutinos.

For a time, numbers of these birds were bred and a few were exhibited alongside the genuine sex-linked Albinos and Lutinos, and it was impossible to be sure of the difference between the two kinds. It is now some years since this composite bird has been bred in this country due, in the main, to the shortage of Fallows needed for setting up the necessary experimental crosses with Cinnamon Whites.

Fallows

When Fallows of many colours were freely available to breeders several handsomely coloured forms were produced, one being the **Opaline Fallow Olive Green** and its **Blue** counterpart. These birds were mainly clear rich orange yellow, or faintly tinted white on their bodies with faint undulations on head and neck and the wing markings and flight feathers medium grey brown. Together with their red eyes, orange beaks and pink legs these Opaline Fallows looked most striking, especially in their Green series.

The first example I bred belonged to the Blue series and was an **Opaline Fallow Cobalt** hen showing just a faint pinkish cobalt suffusion on the lower part of her body. As this hen showed only very faint body colour it caused me to consider the possibility of breeding this composite type in the Dominant Grey form. It was fortunate for me that I had in my breeding stock a Dominant Grey/Opaline Fallow cock which I mated to this particular hen the following season. Amongst their numerous young were three **Opaline Fallow Greys** — two cocks and a hen. The introduction of the Grey character caused the wing markings to be darker and the body colour to be almost completely devoid of any suffusion, giving a clear body effect. Not many of this composite form were bred as few Fanciers had the stock of the right make-up for their creation and the birds themselves were not so colourful as some of the others available at the time. It is now some years since I have seen or heard of a specimen being bred, the last one I produced, and by accident, was about eight years ago. Previous to that, in the 1950's Frank Wait produced several of this particular combination of colours. My own bird was an Opaline Fallow Olive Green hen with quite dark wings and tail and a beautiful golden yellow body shade.

Rainbows

The composite form that has made the greatest impression on Budgerigar breeders over the past decade or two are the **Yellow** or **Golden-faced Opaline Whitewings** and because of their bright and varied coloured plumage are commonly called 'Rainbows'. These birds were first bred and recorded during the first part of 1939 when the three separate mutations concerned with their evolution were beginning to become more widespread through the Fancy. Their breeding was first recorded in an article by myself in the June 1939 Issue of the *Budgerigar Bulletin* No. 50.

Further Types

As indicated, numerous composite colour types can be produced. When breeders look at the range of existing mutations they will at once realise what beautiful and unusually coloured birds can be raised by combining several of these mutations in one bird. Two composite birds of which I have only seen single examples are the **Cinnamon Opaline Greywing Violet Cobalt** and the **Yellow-faced Cinnamon Opaline Slate Whitewing Blue.** The first was a wonderful soft, warm rosy violet pastel shade and the second a rainbow mixture of unusual green and blue shades. The following established mutations will I think help the breeder to plan a programme to produce a specific combination: Yellow, Blue, Greywing, Fallow, Clearwing, Cinnamon, Opaline, Slate, Lacewing, Grey, Dominant Pied, Violet, Clear-flight, Recessive Pied, Yellow-face and Dark.

Standards

It will be seen, by examining the *standards of perfection* for exhibition issued by The Budgerigar Society since its conception, that the outline of Budgerigars has changed considerably. The original Budgerigars were round–headed, streamlined, swift flying, free breeding birds, and their descendants today are the more substantial aviary type and the bold headed, broad shouldered, heavily built exhibition type.

Exhibition birds are bred to display what are known as show properties and because of their build are not so active, free flying, or as prolific as the aviary type. From the exhibition type come the fine proud upstanding beautifully coloured birds that carry their fame to all quarters of the world. The **aviary type** produce the tens of thousands of tame pet Budgerigars, many of which delight their owners by learning to imitate the human voice and other sounds.

There is no other species of bird which gives so much pleasure, comfort and companionship to so many people, in every walk of life, as does the Budgerigar. Since its first importation from Australia in 1840, the Budgerigar has developed in a way beyond all possible expectations for a domesticated species.

Guidelines for Judges and Exhibitors*

Faults and/or defects which should be penalised by judges: Where the word penalised is used, it denotes that a penalty should be applied by a judge, according to his opinion, of the degree of the severity of the faults and/or defects which are before him for consideration. Where a DIRECTIVE is given it must be strictly adhered to.

COMMON TO ALL VARIETIES.

1. CONDITION IS ESSENTIAL. If a bird is not in condition it should be penalised. Perfect show condition is defined as a bird that is in complete feather. Whether it be Yellow or Buff, the feather should show the bloom of good health and good preparation.

2. LONG FLIGHTED. No bird showing long flighted characteristics is eligible to take any award. **(DIRECTIVE)**

3. Birds showing any sign of **SCALYFACE** must be removed from the show bench by the show management on the instruction of the judge. **(DIRECTIVE).** Where possible affected birds should be isolated from the show hall, as should any exhibit which shows signs of sickness and distress.

4. FLECKING is defined as any dark mark (flecks or grizzle) on the crown or frontal of the head, these markings should be penalised severely, bearing in mind that the standard for every variety denotes THE FRONTAL AND CROWN MUST BE CLEAR AND FREE FROM ALL MARKINGS

5. OPALESCENCE. This fault can occur in all varieties where the pattern and distribution of markings is as the normal light green, and is defined as being a visible overlay of body colour intruding on the cheeks, back of the head, neck and wings which detracts from the definition of markings as depicted in the pictorial ideal and described in the colour standards. The varying degree of opalescence must be penalised accordingly.

6. SPOTS. Where applicable in the standards, missing, irregular or badly shaped spots should be penalised, the size of the spots should be in proportion to the rest of the make-up of the bird as is depicted in the pictorial ideal.

7. PRIMARY FLIGHTS. Birds displaying less or more than seven primary flights should be penalised.

8. INHERENT FAULTS. eg. Dropped tail, nipped neck, poor backline, poor deportment, poor wing-carriage, beakiness, etc.... should be penalised.

9. TEMPORARY FAULTS. Missing primary flight or tail feathers, spot feathers (particularly outer spots) and the presence of pin feathers or blood quills should be assessed with due regard to the effect on the overall balance of the exhibit, and should be penalised accordingly.

*These are the rules of judging issued by The Budgerigar Society. Fanciers are advised to obtain the latest information from the Society.

THE MAIN FEATURES OF A BUDGERIGAR

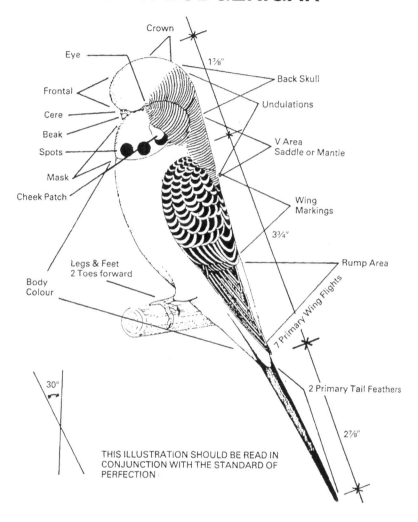

Crown
Eye
Frontal
Cere
Beak
Spots
Mask
Cheek Patch
Legs & Feet
2 Toes forward
Body Colour
1⅞"
Back Skull
Undulations
V Area
Saddle or Mantle
Wing Markings
3¾"
Rump Area
7 Primary Wing Flights
2 Primary Tail Feathers
30°
2⅞"

THIS ILLUSTRATION SHOULD BE READ IN CONJUNCTION WITH THE STANDARD OF PERFECTION

The Modern Budgerigar Standard
Issued by the Budgerigar Society

131

10. ANY DEFORMITY. Should be penalised.

11. BODY COLOUR. Patchiness and/or dilution of body colour above the level of that described in the colour standards and any suffusion of another colour other than that described in the colour standards should be penalised.

FAULTS AND/OR DEFECTS CONFINED TO SPECIFIC VARIETIES,

additional to those listed in guidelines 1 to 11 as above where applicable.

12. ANY VARIETY OPALINE.

WING MARKINGS: The edges of all wing feathers should be well defined and show the same colour as the body, absence of body colour on the wings, smudging or thumb marks of the pattern and distribution of the wing markings should be penalised. MANTLE/ SADDLE should be the same colour as the body and any dark markings in the 'V' area should be penalised, any very heavy dark markings within the area of undulations at the back of the head and neck should also be penalised.

TAILS: Absence of or variegation of solid colour in primary tail feathers should be penalised.

13. NORMAL and OPALINE CINNAMON, NORMAL and OPALINE GREY WING. The body colour in these four varieties should be penalised if it is below or in excess of 50% of the normal body colour in depth and intensity.

14. LUTINO AND ALBINO: The following deviations from the standard should be penalised: pale violet colour in cheek patches, cinnamon brown spots, or markings on the back, wings or tail. suffusion throughout. Albino; there throughout. wings or tail. Lutino; there should be no green Albino; there should be no blue or grey suffusion

15. CLEARWING. (Normal Yellow-wings and Whitewings). The following deviations from the standard should be penalised: dilution of body colour down from approximately the normal depth and intensity; pale violet, pale blue or pale grey cheek patches; absence of blue or grey colour in primary tail feathers; any markings on wings according to the depth of such markings; opalescence on back of head, neck or wings. N.B. Cinnamon Yellow wings and Cinnamon Whitewings must be shown in the A.O.C. classes.

16. CRESTED. An incomplete or damaged circular, half circular or tufted crest should be penalised, and the other faults listed in these guide-lines for whichever variety is carrying the crest should also be considered and penalised accordingly.

17. SPANGLE. The following deviations from the standard should, be penalised: completely black feathers on the wings; incomplete or absent throat spots. DOUBLE FACTOR SPANGLE. Any black or grizzled ticking visible anywhere on the bird, or green, blue or grey suffusion, should be penalised.

18. DOMINANT PIED. The following deviations from the standard should be penalised: an all clear yellow or white body colour: all clear yellow or white wings; spillage of

mask colour around the neck and back of head and the absence of one or more spots.

19. CLEARFLIGHT: The absence of the head patch, broken body colour and/or the presence of dark primary wing or tail feathers should be penalised.

20. RECESSIVE PIED: Dark markings on wings if less than 10% or more than 20% of total area should be penalised. Zebra markings on the frontal should also be penalised bearing in mind that standard for every variety denotes that the FRONTAL AND CROWN SHOULD BE CLEAR AND FREE FROM ALL MARKINGS.

21. DARK-EYED CLEAR YELLOW AND DARK-EYED CLEAR WHITE. Any odd green or blue feathers or green or blue suffusion in the body, or any black or grizzled ticking or suffusion in the wings should be penalised.

22. YELLOWFACE. Mutant 1. Spillage of yellow colour from the mask into the body colour should be penalised; the exception being as described in NOTE 2 of Yellowface and Goldenface mutations Standards.

23. YELLOWFACE Mutant 2 and GOLDENFACE Mutations.
In the double factor form both may display some light spillage of yellow colour into the body colour adjacent to the bottom edge of the mask which is permissible, reference should always be made to the notes 1, 2, and 3, which accompany the written standards for these yellowface mutations

24. LACEWINGS. Incomplete patterns of normal or opaline cinnamon brown markings including primary tail feathers, or any suffusion of green or blue/grey colour into the body colour should be penalised.

25. NORMAL AND OPALINE FALLOWS. A complete absence of body colour should be penalised.

26. WRONG CLASSING OF EXHIBITS. When this is necessary Judges should indicate on the cage label the reason. Where doubt exists, wrong classing should only be carried out after consultation with fellow Judges. The only marks that Judges should make on cage labels are Class Positions, Best of Colour (BOC), Section Awards, Wrong Class (WC) and reason for removal from staging and reason for disqualification. N.B. It is not permitted to indicate the position within the colour line-up.

27. **THE STANDARD OF PERFECTION, SCALE OF POINTS, COLOUR STANDARDS AND PICTORIAL IDEALS AND THESE GUIDELINES**
should all be read in conjunction with each other, they all play a part in
serving as a guide to both Judge and Exhibitor.

28. SHOW CLASSIFICATION. Show schedules can be confusing for inexperienced fanciers, therefore it is advisable that all show promoting societies use the correct description of birds (as defined in the B.S. Colour Standards) when setting out the mandatory show classification, eg. OPALINE CINNAMON (not cinnamon opaline).

APPENDIX

NOTES

BIBLIOGRAPHY

The Cult of the Budgerigar by W. Watmough (Cage Birds, 1935)

The Budgerigar in Bush and Aviary by Neville W. Cayley, FRZS

Naturalists' Miscellany by Shaw and Nodder (1890–1910)

Naturalists' Library by William Jardine and P.J. Selby (1820's)

Birds of Australia and the Adjacent Islands (Lansdowne Press, 1837)

Budgerigars by C.H. Rogers (Bartholomew, Foyle, Gifford and Magna Print, 1970)

Records of Parrots bred in Captivity by Arthur T.A. Prestwick (1952)

Illustrated Natural History by Reverend J.G. Woods

Cassell's Book of Birds by Dr. Brehm (translated by T. Rymer Jones end 19th Century)

The Budgerigar by Dr. Karl Russ (translated end 19th century)

Budgerigars and Cockatiels by C.P. Arthur

Exhibition Budgerigars by Dr. M.D.S. Armour (Cage Birds, 1930)

Lecture on Mendelism by Drinkwater

Mendel's Principles of Heredity by Professor W. Bateson (1905)

Mendelism by R.C. Punnett (1905)

Breeding and the Mendelian Discovery by A.D. Darbishire MA (1911)

Book of Budgerigar Colour Expectations by Dr. H. Duncker and Konsul General Carl H. Cremer (1932, translated by F.S. Elliott)

Incomparable Budgerigars by Percy G. Frudd (1938)

The Budgerigar in Captivity by Denys Weston

Budgerigars and how to breed Cinnamonwings by C.H. Rogers (1934)

The Genetics of the Budgerigar by Prof. F.A.E. Crew and Rowena Lamy (1935)

Budgerigar Matings and Colour Expectations by F.S. Elliott and E.W. Brooks (Budgerigar Society, 1953)

Genetics for Budgerigar Breeders by Taylor and Warner (Illiffe Books, 1961)

NOTES

NOTES

NOTES

NOTES